DECORATING SEWLUTIONS

Learn to Sew as You Decorate Your Home

Donna Babylon

Windsor Oak
PUBLISHING

Library of Congress Cataloging-in-Publication Data

Babylon, Donna.
    Decorating sewlutions : learn to sew as you decorate your home / Donna Babylon.
    p. cm.
    ISBN 987-0-9668227-2-4

1. Sewing. 2. Machine sewing. 3. Textile fabrics in interior decoration. 4. Household linens.
5. House furnishings. 6. Interior decoration –– Amateurs', manuals. I. Title.

TT387 .B33 2010
746.97 20--dc22   2000931468

Cover, Interior Design: Norm Myers
Cover Illustration: Lisa Henderling
Technical Illustrations: Missy Shepler, Ann Davis Mahaffey
Photography: Jim Miller Photography
How-to Photography: Janet Pray, Jessica Johnson, Tammy Ray, Dennis Moore
Editorial Services: Sharon Goldinger of PeopleSpeak
Indexing: Wendy Stegall of Wendex

This book and others published by Windsor Oak Publishing are available at special discounts when purchased in bulk for premiums and sales promotions. Special editions or book excerpts can also be created to specification. For details contact the Special Sales Director at the address below.

Windsor Oak Publishing
P. O. Box 1603
Westminster, MD 21158

For additional information, visit:
MoreSplashThanCash.com

10 9 8 7 6 5 4 3 2 1

Table of Contents

Table of Contents

Recommended Resources:

– CoatsAndClark.com
– Prym-Consumer-USA.com
– HabermanFabrics.com
– RobertAllenDesign.com
– WestminsterFabrics.com
– HeirloomCreations.net

Dear Friends,

True confession: I'm one of them. I'm a "Beck."

That's my abbreviated term of affection for a home economist (full name: Becky Home Eck-y).

Yes, I graduated from college with a degree in home economics. And, yes, I was a home economics teacher for middle and high school students. Back then, in my humble opinion, true-to-the-core Becks took their subject way too seriously (translation: boring!). I, too, took it seriously. However, I was a renegade. I wanted to have too much fun. I saw so many creative possibilities that could come from a sewing machine—and, believe me, none could be classified as boring.

Donna Babylon *Author*

Just imagine teaching 25 to 30 kids (in a classroom) how to sew. Whatever could go wrong did go wrong. I remember one student who unknowingly stitched the shirt she was wearing to the tote bag she was making. Another student intently stitched his project for the entire class only to discover that his machine needle wasn't threaded. And I can't forget the poor student who accidentally cut off the sleeve of her jacket as she was cutting out her project (the jacket was lying on the worktable). I could go on and on.

For my sanity, I quickly learned how to adapt my instructions to bypass any potential problems. When I did that, the classroom was much calmer and my students had immediate success. I felt like a genius! I realized I was onto something—I just didn't know what.

Fast-forward a bunch of years.

The subject of home economics has been eliminated from many school curriculums. If it still exists, it's now called something like "Consumer and Family Sciences." (Does that make me a consumer and family scientist?) Sewing was often the first fatality in this new version of home ec. As a result, many people don't know how to sew! That's why I wrote this book.

I had no idea when I was in the classroom that I would one day be writing how-to books. But when that opportunity presented itself, I decided to write my books the same way I taught—by offering simple and stylish

Meet
HOME DEC BECK

Beck shares her observations, words of wisdom and vaulable tips throughout the book.

projects with well-thought-out instructions. I still see all of the creative opportunities for sewing — especially for the home. And, I still love to teach.

In this book, I have identified 10 projects (which go way beyond totes and potholders) that require only three basic sewing techniques. Every project in this book will make an instant decorating impact on your little corner of the world called home. I did not include anything that might leave you cussing at your sewing machine in frustration. I am giving you the absolute basics necessary for you to be successful but with lots of room to be creative. For example, I give you instructions on how to make a basic pillow. But from those same instructions, you can make a bench cushion for your home or deck, a mattress for a futon, or even a new bed for your favorite furry friend! I encourage you to experiment and explore your newly found talent as a designer and sewer. You'll quickly discover that sewing really is easy.

Since my teaching days, I have had a wonderful career being creative and sharing my love of sewing through the many books and patterns I have written and with the many television appearances and seminars I do around the country. Throughout the process of sculpting my career, I created my own brand: "More Splash Than Cash®." MSTC doesn't mean cheap. It means you do things smarter. It also means that the cash you spend and the time you invest — whatever the amount might be — are well spent and the resulting project will be enjoyed and admired for years — or at least until you get bored with it!

Thanks!

I want to thank everyone who me helped me produce this book, especially my parents who stood by me through thick and thin during this process. Love you so much!

Also, HUGE thanks to Ben Babylon, Tammy "Toby" Ray, Sandra Hughes of Sew Custom Treatments of Wakefield, Inc., Sheila Zent, Bo and Donna Darr, Ray Wentz, Brenda Stonesifer, Donna Taylor, Cary Pierson, Suzanne Dell, Rita Farro, Linda Griepentrog, Wendy Hevey, Jean Fidler, Maggie Warner, Carol Johnson, Janet Pray, Jessica Johnson, Alice Haupt, Mary Hicks, Maureen Klein, Greg Smith, Toby Haberman, Ann, Jordon, Katie, Jonah, Luke, Curtis, Nick, and Justin.

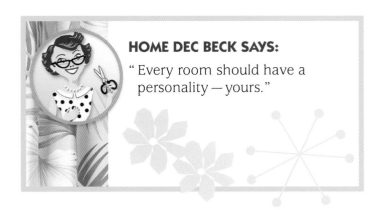

HOME DEC BECK SAYS:

" Every room should have a personality — yours."

Signature Style Decorating

No matter where you live, whether it is a one-room studio apartment or a mansion, your home should be a reflection of you. The biggest question before starting any decorating project is usually "Where do I begin?" It might sound odd, but decorating really begins with you and your innate sense of style — not with the color of the walls or the fabric you choose (that will come in time). You are probably more aware of your fashion style than your decorating style. Just as your fashion style, your sense of decorating style has also developed through your life experiences (and it will continue to evolve throughout the years). Decorating comes from your personal perspective, and this individuality should be stamped on every room in your home. This is your "signature style," and it's what makes your home unique.

Muse Views

Through many sources, we are bombarded with images and information of prelabeled decorating styles — Urban Chic, Retro, Cottage, Traditional, French Country to name a few. These "labeled styles" can be intimidating, confusing, and most importantly, very impersonal.

Don't get me wrong. These style suggestions are a good basis for your decorating decisions, but they don't have to be copied exactly. Critique what you see and make a mental note of why or why not it appeals to you. By exposing yourself to as many of these different labeled decorating styles as possible, you will gain confidence in relying on your signature style.

Get Real

Do you really want your home to look like a magazine photo? What happens to this perfect and pristine room if you spill coffee on your white sofa? Or when your cat throws up on the carpet? Or, when someone brings mud into the kitchen after a hike in the woods? Don't forget that you are decorating for real life — not a photo shoot. So make your plans to let the chips fall between the cushions!

Basic Instincts

As you go about making your decorating decisions, don't doubt your instincts. Your initial reaction to a piece of furniture, fabric, or paint color is usually the right one. If you think the fabric is too delicate or the sofa is too large, it probably is. If you compromise your instinctive reaction and settle for something that you are not happy with for whatever reason, you will be disappointed in the long run.

Take a Survey of Your Life

Before you make any decorating decisions, take note of the way you live, the way you relax, the way you entertain, and your likes and dislikes. The answers to the following questions will have a direct impact on refining your signature style. By answering the following questions honestly (there are no right or wrong answers), your thoughts will be more focused when it comes to creating a customized decorating plan that you will be happy with.

Discuss the questions with others who share your home so that you can all be in agreement with your decorating efforts. Consider your answers when selecting fabrics, arranging furniture, and accessorizing your home.

Lifestyle Survey

Here's a sampling of key questions to get you started:

How many people live with you?   _____

Number of adults: _____

Number of children: _____

Do you watch a lot of television?   _____
    Alone? As a family? With friends?

Is your home a gathering place for your kids' friends?   _____

Do you have pets?   _____

Do they have unlimited access to your home?   _____

Where do you eat your meals?   _____
    In front of the television? At the kitchen table?
    In bed? Standing at the stove with fork in hand?

Do you have enough storage space?   _____

What kind of storage do you need?   _____

For what kinds of stuff?   _____

Do you have a hobby that requires a large work area?   _____

Do you need a designated space for this activity?   _____

Do you entertain?   _____
    How often?

Do you have large or small parties?   _____

Do you work out of your home?   _____

Can your home office be incorporated into an
    existing room designated for another use or
    do you need a separate space?   _____

What room do you want to decorate first?   _____

Why?   _____

PART 1: Plan It!

Decorating does not have to be expensive. With a basic understanding of fabric, color, and furniture arranging, you can easily decorate your home exactly the way you want it — even on the tightest of budgets. This section provides you with lots of information to begin any decorating project with total confidence.

TABLE OF CONTENTS:

Your Design Direction

Okay, let's review. You've settled on your road-map fabric — check. You've selected all of the coordinating fabrics — check. You've picked the wall color, floor color and accent color — check, check, and, check. The colors are distributed evenly around the room, and you've drawn a kick-ass floor plan and furniture arrangement. You are so good!

Now, to keep all of your thoughts together in one cohesive spot, create a comprehensive "style board" that will show all your selections in one place so that you can execute your decorating plan in an efficient manner. Besides, it is such a "designer" thing to do!

Gather Together

Even though actual samples of the following are best, don't freak out if you can't get an actual sample. Pictures from catalogs or magazines will also work. Note: Get the largest sizes possible of all the samples; try to keep the size of the sample in proportion to the amount it will be seen in the room. Some samples are free, you may have to purchase others. Gather together the samples you need for your room. Some suggestions include:

- Road-map fabric
- Coordinating fabric
- Geometric fabric
- Accent color fabric
- Carpet sample
- Tile sample
- Countertop sample
- Wallpaper border sample
- Decorative trim
- Wall color paint
- Piece of wallpaper (large enough to cover foam board surface)
- Large paint chip of trim paint color
- Large paint chip of ceiling paint color

Also gather together:

- White foam core board
- Paintbrush
- Glue
- Scissors

I've gathered together paint, fabric, and carpet samples to see how they work together. After I make my final decision, I will make a style board to carry with me as I complete my room.

Follow the instructions below to construct your style board.

1. Paint both sides of the foam board with your selected wall color (if you only paint one side, the board will warp). Or attach wallpaper to one side of the board with glue.

2. Place a copy of your floor plan at the top and center of the board. Attach your room measurements and dimensions you have collected to the back of the board.

3. Arrange all of your samples in the general order of the room. For example, place the carpet sample at the bottom edge of the board, the fabric samples in the middle, and paint chips for the ceiling and trim near the top of the board. This will give you a much clearer picture than sticking samples randomly over the board.

4. Take pictures of the lighting fixtures, furniture, and so on that you plan to use and include them in the arrangement.

5. When the arrangement is pleasing to your eye, glue everything in place.

6. Label all of the samples to show what they are being used for. Identify what fabric is going to be used for the curtains, throw pillows, throw, duvet cover, table runner, and so on.

Live with Your Style Board

Once you have assembled all the items on your board, prop it up against the wall in the room it is intended for. Look at it as you enter or leave the room and at different times during the day. Leave it up until you feel you have a complete picture of the end result. Ask yourself,

- Do you like the color combination?

- Does anything look out of place?

- Are you happy with the proportions and distribution of colors and fabrics?

- Does the scale of the patterns work together?

- Do you have enough texture included in your plans?

Feel free to remove or replace any pieces until you are completely satisfied. Keep your style board handy and take it with you when you are shopping to match all of your selections.

"Use these simple suggestions and you will
see your home in a whole new light."

1 | Design for Living

**Most of these
suggestions are
inexpensive to
incorporate into
your decorating
plans. In fact,
most are
downright free!**

Decorating is fun, creative, and expressive. I don't want you
to feel overwhelmed about any of the decisions you have
to make. If you follow these 14 easy steps, decorating your
space is sure to be a rewarding experience. And these suggestions will help you stay within your budget. Most of
these steps are inexpensive to complete. In fact, most are
downright free!

Step 1: Clean Up Your Clutter

Too much stuff and not enough places to keep it organized
and out-of-sight is a universal problem—not just for everyday living conditions but also for effective decorating decisions. Why? Because it is difficult to make objective observations and see a room's potential and its pitfalls if it is in
constant disarray. The bottom line is you need to eliminate
clutter before you begin to decorate.

Be honest as you begin this process. Are you really going to
have time to read the stack of magazines that have been
collecting for three years? Get rid of them! The same goes
for the dilapidated chair that no one can safely sit in. Be
firm and disciplined with yourself about your commitment
to get rid of the clutter and any unwanted items. Realisti-
cally, though, you may have sentimental items that you
don't want to get rid of. That's understandable and perfectly OKAY. The purpose of this exercise is not to throw
away your personal history but to eliminate clutter.

Step 2: Perfection on Paper

An accurate floor plan can help you plan how much material (paint, wallpaper, and carpeting, for example) you need
to successfully complete your project. A floor plan is the

outline of a room's parameters that indicates accurate sizes and placement of everything in the room including windows, doors, radiators, baseboards, fireplaces, vents, electric outlets, light switches and built-in bookshelves.

Floor plans are a handy resource when buying new or rearranging existing furniture. Imagine your frustration when your brand new sofa arrives and it doesn't fit through the door. A room plan drawn to scale will prevent this situation. Floor plans allow you to experiment with different furniture arrangements and to plan the best traffic flow around the room without breaking your back moving furniture.

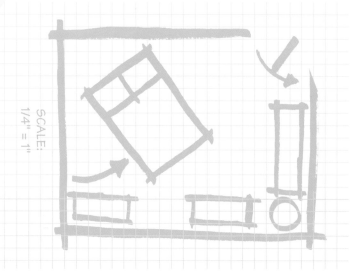

SCALE: 1/4" = 1'

Measure your furniture to make sure it fits in your space.

Step 3: Embrace Your Space

Rooms come in all shapes and sizes. Keep in mind that what's important is not the size of the room but the way you use the space. Apply common sense to any decision, and focus on the comfort and convenience of your family. Create a room that seems to invite you in and hopes you stay for a while. For example, imagine a living room that beckons you home from a hard day at work, a dining room that encourages your friends to linger, and a bedroom that you'll hate to get out of — even on the brightest of Saturday mornings!

Walk This Way

Traffic should flow logically around and through the room. Traffic lanes between the most-used

Allow at least 18" between the coffee table and sofa.

pieces should be kept as clear as possible, and the traffic path should be at least $2^1/_2$ feet wide. Since doorways usually dictate the traffic flow from one room to another; the traffic lane should be the most direct route. If you are lazy like me, you don't want to take any extra steps going from one room to another — especially if you're on the way to the fridge for a snack! This means you don't want any large pieces of furniture in the way. Work out any potential problems like this on paper before moving any furniture.

Step 4: Find Your Focus

A room will feel much more inviting if you arrange the furniture around what is called a "focal point." A focal point should be the first thing you want to see when entering a room (it's usually the largest architectural feature in the room). An architectural feature could be a fireplace, a picture window, or a built-in wall unit such as a bookcase.

If your room is lacking an architectural focal point, then you can create one with a large piece of furniture, such as an armoire or an entertainment center. The mere size will command visual attention that creates the focal point. Another way to increase attention to the focal point is to paint the wall behind it a rich and vibrant paint color.

Step 5: Making Arrangements

Use scaled paper furniture templates to arrange a room directly on your floor plan. Move the furniture around by lifting merely a finger! You'll see at a glance whether or not the furniture will fit, where it will be the most functional, and where the traffic paths in the room have to be kept clear.

Use the following suggestions for arranging furniture in your room.

- Place the first piece of furniture in the room for the primary activity of the room—the sofa in the living room, the bed in the bedroom, or the desk in the office. This piece of furniture should address or face the focal point.

- Next, place pieces that relate to or connect with the main piece for comfort and convenience. For example, a chair in the living room needs to connect with the sofa and coffee table. Nightstands in the bedroom need to connect with the bed.

- Now place the remaining pieces of furniture from the largest to the smallest.

A U-shaped seating arrangement is perfect for easy conversation.

- Arrange the seating in a U-shape that faces the focal point. This arrangement softens the formality of a room and gives the room a sense of liveliness.

- Think vertical if you're decorating a small room. Add tall pieces such as a bookshelf, an entertainment center, or an armoire to take your eye off the smallness of the room. Floor-length curtains are a better choice than valances because they create a tall visual line.

- If your room is narrow, place the main piece of furniture against the narrow wall. Then add smaller pieces in some variation of the U shape. Furniture pieces placed diagonally in a corner will create an illusion of width.

- Don't place all of the furniture around the perimeter of the room or directly against the walls. This dance-floor style of furniture arranging is cold and uninviting.

- Consider dividing a large room into small "minirooms." These minirooms can be defined with area rugs. Adding an additional conversa-tion area or another table and chairs builds flexibility into a room.

Step 6: Hues You Can Use

This next statement may not sit well with art teachers and designers, but oh heck, I'll say it anyway: Throw away the color wheel. (I can hear the screams of disbelief now!) Let me explain my logic. You don't need to get hung up on whether your color scheme is monochromatic or analogous (if you don't know what these terms mean, that's exactly my point). The professionals who design fabrics have this technical knowledge, and we benefit from their color expertise and choices. They did the work for us and determined a beautiful color palette. What is important is to be aware of the emotional and physical impact color has on the rooms we decorate. This will be discussed in more detail in chapter 2, "Escape from Beigeland."

Step 7: A Masterful Mix

Think of fabrics as the decorating personality that you buy by the yard. Fabrics are what bring the room to life. The fabric's design, the way it drapes, and how and where it is used all contribute to the character of the room.

When placing fabrics around the room, don't cluster the same fabrics in one part of the room. Spread them around to give the room visual balance. Otherwise, the room will look lopsided.

Step 8: Texture Lecture

Everything in the room has texture; the key is to have enough different textures to make the room interesting without going over the top. Think of all the features in

Incorporate interesting textures with a variety of accessories.

your room and their innate texture (including the floor and walls). The challenge is to avoid having too much of the same texture. A room full of upholstered furniture pieces is BOOOORing. In the same way, a room full of all-wood furniture on a wood floor will bring on a yawn every time.

Step 9: Go Vertical

A common problem for DIY decorators is the tendency to decorate from eye level down. This creates an awkward, bottom-heavy feel to the room, and your eye won't find it very interesting. The good news is it's easy to add height to your room with floor length curtains, picture arrangements, etc.

Step 10: Balancing Act

You'll know when you have a well-decorated room because it will *feel* balanced and not like you're on the Titanic (because everything is being pulled to one side as if you are sinking). The room will feel welcoming because the furniture, art, and accessories (including window treatments) are varied in size, shape, texture and height. The room will entertain your eye because the color and accessories are distributed around the room. All of the elements in a room are connected, both visually and physically.

Step 11: Windows of Opportunity

Window treatments have a lot of responsibilities. When they are opened, they beckon us to come outside to enjoy the fresh air. However, when closed, they make you feel protected from any harsh elements of nature. The main job of a window treatment is to provide security and privacy from the outside world. Do you love the light as a new day breaks? That's great! But you probably don't want to live in a fishbowl, especially at night. The window treatment you choose should satisfy both situations.

At the same time, you can't ignore the fact that window treatments contribute greatly to the style of the room. Whether you want the clean lines of a Roman shade, the softness that a floor-length curtain provides, or the exclamation point of color that you can get from a valance, window treatments are an important component to successful decorating. Plan accordingly.

Step 12: Art Smarts

You may have heard that you should hang artwork so the center of the picture is at eye level. Right away you may be confused. Whose eye level? Yours or someone else who is over 6 feet tall? Okay,

This picture is too small for the space and placed too high over the bed.

here's the deal. If you are hanging art in a room where you will mainly be standing (as in an entryway or hallway), hang the artwork so the center point of the art is 60 to 65 inches from the floor. But if you are hanging art in a room where you generally sit down (a dining room, family room, or office), hang the pictures a few inches lower.

If artwork is placed directly over a piece of furniture, hang it so the bottom of the frame is positioned about 6 inches above the top of the sofa back or tabletop so it doesn't look like a UFO. When grouping pictures together contain them within an invisible geometric shape such as a rectangle so the bottom row of frames is arranged in a straight line.

Step 13: The Guiding Light

Lighting can add drama and atmosphere to a room. Think about each area of your room and choose lighting to match the function of the space. Don't rely on a central ceiling light as your only light source. Instead, use a variety of different sources, such as recessed spotlights, task lighting, track lighting, table, desk, and floor lamps (perhaps with dimmer switches), and uplighters.

Step 14: Take Your Time

Decorating is an ongoing process. Simply accept that your room will never be completely finished. So be patient and enjoy the journey.

"I've loved color ever since I opened my first box of crayons. And I still love to color outside the lines!"

2 | Escape from Beigeland

A room can't be decorated without color. Because color affects the mood of the room and the emotions of its occupants, the choice of color in a room is a major key to decorating success.

We see so many colors all around us. But when it comes to selecting and committing to colors to live with, the final decision can be overwhelming. So we hesitate. Or we'll pick the same old boring beige that was originally on the walls because it is safe and you know what to expect. This chapter will help you get over the hesitation hump and release you from beigeland. After applying even a few of these tips, you will have more confidence when selecting colors so that this aspect of decorating will be fun and not dreaded.

Colorful Thoughts

As I promised before, we are not going to get involved with the color wheel. However, the color concepts I think you should understand are hue, value, temperature, and intensity. This is the simplified version.

- Hue is just another word for color and is used interchangeably.

- Value refers to the lightness or darkness of a color. Lighter colors are usually referred to as "pastels."

- Colors are divided into two temperatures: warm and cool. Yellows, reds, and oranges are associated with heat and are considered to be "warm" colors (think of a fire). Greens, blues, and violets remind us of forests, lakes, morning mist, and snowcapped mountains. They are considered to be "cool" colors.

- Intensity is about the brightness or dullness of a color. These are the colors that actually set the mood of a room. The intensity of colors can be bright and vivid (think of a lemon) or quiet and understated (think of an evergreen tree).

Color Clues

There are many different ways to plan a color scheme, but this is my favorite. Study the fabrics carefully. What are the three main colors in the fabric? Consider using one of the colors for the wall color, the other for the floor color. Use the third color as the accent color. There's your color scheme!

Something amazing happens to your room when color is added: the room comes to life—reflecting your style, creating a cohesive look, and generating a personality all its own. However, don't be too literal when selecting your wall color; the shades can be darker or lighter than what is in your fabric. But before making a final decision, learn how the color you chose affects the mood of the room.

You will find that no two people's reactions to color are exactly the same. In fact, if two people are shown the same color, let's say, pale blue, their responses could be completely opposite. One

In Living Color

There are no right and wrong color choices when decorating the different rooms in your

home. But wall color is more than visual fizz—it has a direct affect on the mood of its occupants. After you have determined the purpose and function of the room you are decorating, consider the following color characteristics to create the perfect mood for your home.

Living/Family Room – Any warm color is a good choice for this room. Shades of pink and peach encourage people to be more social whereas deep oranges (rust) and rich

browns provide a feeling of comfort and security. When brown is combined with its first cousin, beige, the room will be unpreten-

tious and comfortable to live in. Greens are associated with calmness, safety, comfort, and relaxation—all characteristics desirable in a room where family and friends gather.

Dining Room – Dark red is an interesting choice for a dining area, especially if you entertain a lot because it encourages conversation and appetite. Rich red is associated with sophistication. White walls in a dining

room do not create an intimate feeling. Brown elicits thoughts of delicious food, such as chocolate, brownies, fudge, and cappuccino. Shades of orange will stimulate the appetite.

Kitchen – Bright and cheery pinks used as accents (for example, tabletop accessories like place mats and dinnerware) can create a playful mood. Yellow

suggests delicious and fresh foods and is a nice choice for a kitchen. If you are dieting, know that bright orange is an appetite stimulant. Blue is the least appetizing of all colors (who likes blue food?) and is not recommended for kitchens for this reason.

Den/Study – Deep blues are perfect for dens and reading nooks because it encourages meditative thinking. Deep, rich reds are also a good choice for this room, which is many times decorated to create a masculine feel. Traditional red is also at home in a den (think beautiful tartan fabrics).

Home Office – Blue may create a too relaxing atmosphere for an office, especially if you have deadlines to meet. Consider green instead because it encourages concentration. Lemon, jasmine, and golden yellows unleash creative juices.

Children's Room/Nursery – Girls' rooms do not have to be pink, and boys' rooms do not have to be blue. Blue has a calming effect on all children. Lavender has always been a girly-girl color. Not too many boys want a lavender bedroom. Bright pinks stimulate imagination and creativity and bright purple gives a feeling of fun, adventure, and the

person's response could be "That reminds me of a perfect summer sky," whereas the other person may say, "That reminds me of a cold winter day." Either response is right and can be used effectively in decorating, but it just goes to show that color choice is a very personal decision.

Natural and artificial lighting affect color immensely. This means that the colors you select for your room will look completely different in the morning than they will in the evening and

even throughout the day. To be sure that you are making good color choices, bring samples of all components you are thinking of using into the room (paint, carpet, wallpaper, fabrics, etc.) and observe them for a few days. If they work together at all times, and you like what you see, that's great. Proceed with confidence and a smug smile. However, if even one item doesn't look right to your eye, now is the time to make changes until you are completely satisfied.

unexpected. Being exposed to yellow for long periods of time can irritate people and make them easily provoked. It may not be the best choice in rooms that are shared.

Nursery – Red is the first color that captures a baby's attention. However, using large doses of

this color in a nursery can be overstimulating to a baby. Using red accents may be a better approach. In some studies, it was determined that yellow agitates babies and makes them cry. The lighter shades of orange or green are a good compromise color.

Bathrooms/Powder Rooms – Blue is a natural color to decorate in rooms where water is used, and it's an excellent choice for bathrooms where you want to enjoy long, relaxing soaks. For a spa like feeling, soft yellow-greens (sage) and blue-greens (aqua) are good choices. Lavender can have the same calming effects as blue. Soft pinks and peaches bring out the natural glow of any skin tones, but yellow has the opposite effect.

Bedrooms – To evoke a peaceful feeling in a bedroom, select a shade of green (the color associated with comfort and relaxation). Blues and purples are also calming—and sophisticated. Blue-greens, such as teal and aqua, are great

stress-relieving colors. Even though red is considered to be the sexiest of all colors, too much red in the bedroom can become tiring. Accents in deep reds are a better option. Pinks are warm, inviting, and romantic, whereas shades of purple are spiritual in nature.

Hallways/Entryways – Red can exude all its glory in these areas because people pass through them quickly. It is a bold and fresh welcome to all who enter. Yellow is an interesting choice for these areas of the home, especially when natural light is nonexistent. Pale peach is a welcoming color — perfect for inviting guests into your home.

A Note about Black and White – Black evokes many diverse reactions and feelings. It can

seem arty, deathly, empowering, sinister, sexy, and anything in between. Most people agree that too much black in a room would be too dark and depressing. However, black can add elegance and sophistication to any room when it's used for carefully selected accessories, floor coverings, and furniture pieces.

An all-white room can come across as being sterile, cold, and inhospitable. However, white trim adds a crisp finishing touch and can outline and define shapes within a room. A white ceiling can act as a visual advantage in small, dark spaces and rooms.

Connected by Color

A well decorated home has what is called "color continuity," especially in the "public" rooms where the colors flow from one room to another.

A public room is a room that people other than the residents see (for example, the hallway, living room, dining room, kitchen). Color is what creates the continuity between these rooms. In the private, individual rooms of your home (your master bedroom, the children's rooms, etc.), you can decorate with different colors that don't have to flow together. Here are some ways to connect the rooms:

- The easiest way to create color continuity is to use the same color on all of the walls in adjoining rooms. This can be accomplished with paint, wallpaper, and even paneling. Once you

Pick the Perfect Palette

Write the very first color that comes to mind to the following questions. This exercise will help you narrow down your color choices and make your decorating decisions easier. What color would you like to be surrounded with when

- you wake up in the morning? _____
- you take a shower? _____
- you take a relaxing bath? _____
- you prepare meals? _____
- you relax? _____
- you work on your favorite hobby? _____
- you pay bills? _____
- you eat dinner? _____

What is the last color you would like to see before closing your eyes and going to sleep? _____

What color would you not like to have as a main color in any room of your home? _____

have this uniformity, take each room in different directions with fabric choices, art, area rugs and trim color.

- If you want to have different wall colors in adjoining rooms (and no one says you can't), the secret is to select colors of the same value. This way, one room will not scream for more attention than the others.

- Choose one floor covering and use it throughout the same living level to create an easy visual flow from room to room. Then define a "room within a room" with area rugs.

- Use the same fabric for window treatments in rooms that flow into each other. The style of the window treatment does not have to be the same, just the fabric.

Color Magic

One of color's greatest attributes is its ability to "fool the eye." A coat of paint can create what seems like magic and make a room appear larger, smaller, narrower, or wider. Use these special effects on your walls to your advantage:

- To make a small room appear larger, paint the walls and trim in a light, cool color.

- To make a large room appear smaller, select a medium-dark color that visually causes the walls to "advance" and creates the illusion of a smaller and cozier room.

- For the same reason, use a medium-dark color on a high ceiling to make it appear lower. On the flip side, to make a ceiling appear higher, paint it white.

- To shorten a long, narrow room, paint the short end walls a warm, dark color. This will create the illusion that the walls are advancing and being "pulled together." Paint the longer walls a light hue to make them visually recede.

- Unify walls that are broken up by doorways and windows by painting any wood trim the same color as the walls.

PART 1
PLAN IT!

HOME DEC BECK SAYS:

"Sometimes it's okay to be materialistic."

3 | *Material Pleasures*

Fabric's main function is to add color, pattern and texture to a room.

Fabrics create the decorating personality of any room. In fact, great decorating schemes start with fabric. The spirit of the fabrics and the way they are used together are what give a room character. Fabric's main function is to add color, pattern, and texture and to soften the hard edges of furniture and architectural features.

Material Mix

Want to combine fabrics like the designers do? Follow these easy tips and you'll become a pro! You can decorate a room with fabulous results using just two or three fabrics.

- Begin by walking through the aisles of a fabric store, looking for a fabric to fall in love with. When you find the one (you'll just know it), this fabric becomes what I call your "road map" for all of your future decorating decisions. You may have also heard the terms "inspiration fabric," or "key fabric," which means the same. This road-map fabric

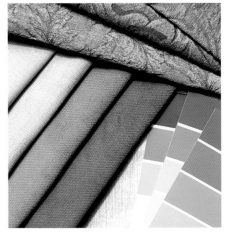

11

will be the predominant fabric in the room (use it at least three times). After you determine your road-map fabric, you are ready to finish creating your room.

- For an interesting fabric combination, vary the style and scale of the fabric designs — do not choose all plaids, florals, or geometrics. Instead, mix the fabric choices to include large, small, or medium prints and geometric designs (checks, plaids, circles, dots, or stripes).

- All colors in the "road map" fabric do not have to be in the coordinating fabrics. However, the fabrics should be united by at least three of the most dominant colors. Also, pay attention to the background colors (also referred to as the "ground" color) as they, too, need to blend. For example, if you're using fabrics with the same background color, such as an off-white, make sure the off-whites match.

Natural Goodness

When it comes to protecting the earth and the environment, your everyday choices matter. Whether you've already been making conscious decisions for a while or are just starting to think green, it's fun to explore eco-friendly decorating options. You certainly don't have to sacrifice style to keep your promise to be earth-friendly when sewing for your home. Today you can find a flourishing selection of beautiful and environmentally responsible textiles. Luckily, plenty of natural fibers can be used to make these fabrics. Some of the more popular fibers are organic cotton, hemp, jute, and bamboo.

Organic Cotton

Organic cotton is grown in soil that is certified to be free of chemical fertilizers and pesticides for at least three years. The fiber can be as soft as traditional cotton and, as an added bonus, it will not irritate your skin because it is free of chemicals.

Hemp

Hemp plants are extremely hardy and require few pesticides to ward off weeds and bugs. Fabrics made from hemp can be as soft as cotton, as sturdy as denim, and as flowing as linen.

Jute (Also Known as Burlap)

The jute plant takes only 4 to 5 months to reach maturity, which makes it highly sustainable and quickly renewable. Jute fibers can be woven into fabric that has a natural earthy color and silk-like luster.

Bamboo

Bamboo is a grass that grows extremely fast (it can be harvested in only 3 years) and without the use of pesticides and fertilizers. It never requires replanting because of its extensive root system. Bamboo fabric is surprisingly soft to the touch and is often compared to cashmere and silk in that regard.

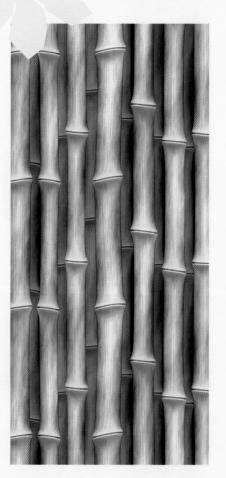

- When selecting prints, be aware of any existing architectural patterns in your room like tiled or parquet floors, circular windows, or arched doors. All of these elements have a definite pattern that will need to blend with any additional patterns you introduce.

- Also consider the texture of the fabric — both visual and tactile. Visual texture is interesting to look at, whereas tactile texture is what you can actually feel with your hand. Fabric choices contribute to both tactile and visual texture. Fabrics with interesting textures include faux suede, silk, chenille, linen, velvet, and chintz. Embroidery also adds texture.

An easy two-fabric combination is a geometric fabric (such a stripe, check, or plaid) teamed with a print with similar colors.

An easy three-fabric combination is a large print or geometric fabric and two solid color fabrics. ▶

Include fabrics with interesting textures in your fabric scheme. ◀

Selecting Fabrics You Can Live With

Consider your lifestyle and your roommates (children and pets included) when choosing fabrics and how you plan to use them. You don't want to be fretting constantly if grape juice or red wine spills will stain your furniture. Here are some guidelines to select fabrics that you can live with.

- Light, solid-colored fabrics show dirt and soil whereas dark-colored fabrics show debris (think pet hair). A better choice may be a medium, multicolored and textured pattern that will hide many forgotten chocolate chip cookies!

- Dark, matte colors absorb light, whereas shiny fabrics reflect light. This is important if you are trying to brighten a dark room.

- All fabrics will fade over time — especially when exposed to continuous sunlight. Fading is more noticeable in darker colors than with lighter colors. Blues (including purples) and reds are particularly susceptible to fading.

- Textured and napped fabrics have uneven surfaces that can trap dirt, feel scratchy to bare legs, and wear unevenly.

- Denim is durable for children's and family rooms. Though most often thought of as blue, denim can be dyed many colors, including black and red.

PART 1
PLAN IT!

HOME DEC BECK SAYS:

"You will never regret buying a neutral sofa or chair because you can instantly update your décor with new and colorful accessories"

- To judge a fabric for durability, keep in mind the tighter the weave, the longer the wear. To check the weave of a fabric, hold it up to the light. The less light that shows through, the tighter the weave is.

- If you use neutral-colored fabrics on upholstered furniture pieces, it will be easier to change the look and feel of the room with colorful accents such as throw pillows, window treatments, area rugs, and other accessories.

Material Differences

You don't have to be a detective when selecting fabrics for your projects as the fabrics themselves offer helpful clues for decorating decisions. Most fabrics widths are 45 or 48 or 54 to 60 inches wide. Fabrics specifically for decorating are usually 54 inches wide or wider. Fabrics used for clothing, quilts, and crafts are usually 45 or 48 inches wide. Specialty fabrics can be up to 100 inches wide or more.

54-inch-wide Decorator Fabrics

- Designs printed on decorator fabrics repeat at regular intervals along both side edges (the selvages). This interval is known as the pattern repeat. When fabric widths are sewn together for larger projects (such as a duvet cover, shower curtain, or curtains), the designs can be matched so the pattern is uninterrupted. This feature is not found on fabrics for making clothing, quilts, or crafts.

- If your fabric has a pattern repeat, you will need extra fabric so you can match the design at the seams. You figure this amount while doing fabric calculations for the project you are making. The larger the pattern, the larger the repeat, therefore, the more fabric you will need.

- The distance between the same design can be anywhere from 3 inches to a yard or more. Don't be upset about having to purchase this extra fabric—you'll be pleasantly surprised by how many other smaller projects you can make with the leftover fabric. Throw pillows and place mats, for example, don't take a lot of fabric.

- On the selvage (the tightly woven finished edge) of printed fabrics you'll find the selvage "legend" that includes a line of colored circles or squares, the designer's and/or manufacturer's name, and usually a "plus" sign to indicate where the repeat begins. Ignore everything except the plus sign. This mark is helpful to determine repeat sizes when calculating yard-

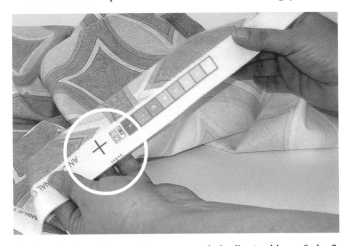

The beginning of a pattern repeat is indicated by a "plus" sign on the selvage.

PART 1 PLAN IT!

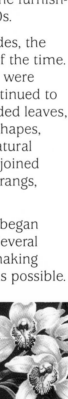

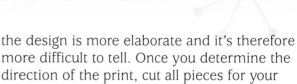

PART 1
PLAN IT!

What Is Bark Cloth?
"'Splain it to me, Lucy!"

Bark cloth has a very interesting history. This is the short version.

Bark cloth was originally made from the bark of trees. Today the term refers to a medium-weight fabric whose texture resembles that of tree bark.

The fabric is surprisingly soft, with a nice drape, which makes it an ideal choice for curtains. It is also quite durable and can be used successfully as an upholstery fabric. The fabric was used extensively for curtains and other home furnishings from the 1930s through the 1960s.

As the fabric evolved during the decades, the designs reflected the popular motifs of the time. In the '30s, floral and tropical designs were prevalent. By the '40s, the fabrics continued to feature tropical designs but also included leaves, birds, old-fashioned scenes, abstract shapes, and delicate florals. In the '50s, the natural elements of leaves and feathers were joined with geometric motifs such as boomerangs, flying saucers, and cocktail glasses.

Interest in decorating with bark cloth began again the '80s, and continues today. Several companies manufacture bark cloth, making sure that the motifs are as authentic as possible.

age for your project. Solid-colored fabrics do not have anything printed on the selvages.

- Many fabric designs are designed with a specific top and bottom. You need to identify the top of the design so your project is cut correctly. Study the fabric to determine the direction of the print. Many designs are obvious (trees should always be upright, for example) but many times

the design is more elaborate and it's therefore more difficult to tell. Once you determine the direction of the print, cut all pieces for your project in the same direction.

- Special protective finishes are applied to decorator fabrics to resist wrinkles, mildew, soiling, fading, and overall deterioration, to name a few. Many times they are indicated on a tag that is

PART 1
PLAN IT!

HOME DEC BECK SAYS:

" At the store, roll a few yards of decorator fabric off the tube to see if the design is printed on the grain. Bring the selvages together, and fold the fabric to see if it lies flat without any ripples and the motifs match (ripples at the fold area indicates the fabric is not printed on grain). If the fabric doesn't do this, and it is off more than 1 inch, consider using another fabric. It's just not worth the headache!"

Size Matters

Here's a handy reference chart that lists how many inches are in each portion of a yard.

Yards	Inches
$1/8$ yard	$4^1/2$ inches
$1/4$ yard	9 inches
$1/3$ yard	12 inches
$3/8$ yard	$13^1/2$ inches
$1/2$ yard	18 inches
$5/8$ yard	$22^1/2$ inches
$2/3$ yard	24 inches
$3/4$ yard	27 inches
$7/8$ yard	$31^1/2$ inches
1 yard	36 inches

attached to the fabric roll. These finishes make these fabrics more expensive but are beneficial characteristics when making home décor projects.

- Dry-cleaning is recommended for most decorator fabrics to maintain their original qualities. Consider the care and upkeep of the fabric you are considering—and your lifestyle—before you make your final decision.

45-inch-wide
Cotton Fabrics

Many beautiful fabrics are available in this width from amazing designers. Keep in mind that these

fabrics are not available for as long as decorator fabrics are; they can change every 6 to 9 months. Be sure to purchase enough fabric for a room at the same time to avoid disappointment at not being able to find the fabric and its coordinates later. These fabrics are displayed on bolts; they are folded in half so you only see 22 inches of the design. Open the fabric up so you can see the entire design.

Fabrics typically used for crafts, quilts, and fashion don't have the special finishes that are found on decorator fabrics (meaning most of these fabrics can be washed).The designs will not match when fabric widths are stitched together because their printing process is different. You can choose to ignore this, or you can camouflage it by stitching a flat trim over the seam. You may come across 45-inch-wide fabrics that are labeled "decorator fabrics." These fabrics are similar in weight to decorator fabrics, but they do not have the special protective finishes found on their 54-inch counterparts nor can you match the designs at the seams.

"When I go fabric shopping, I always feel like a kid in a candy store. I want everything!"

4 | Shop 'til You Drop!

**PART 1
PLAN IT!**

Shopping for fabric is a creative adventure. And finding the perfect fabric for your project is like falling in love for the first time.

To me, nothing is more exciting than selecting the fabric for a project. Ever since I started sewing, I have been addicted to fabrics. I walk the fabric aisles (of any fabric store I can find) with my arms outstretched so my fingers can touch the fabrics. I can spend hours doing this! Fabric inspires me. It seduces me. It "talks" to me. It tells me what I should make from it. It's the main reason I sew. Once I was teaching a class and as I was arranging the fabric on the table, the students commented that they could tell how much I loved fabric because of the way I touched it. It was kind of embarrassing, but at the same time, it was true.

Navigating a Fabric Store

Fabrics in a general fabric store are usually arranged by suggested use categories: fashion, bridal and special occasion, decorating, crafts, and quilting. Specialty fabric stores, such as a quilt store or decorator

fabric store, have lots of fabric to choose from, all with similar characteristics. For example:

- A quilt store features 100 per-cent cotton fabrics that are typically 45 inches wide.

- A decorator fabric store has mostly 54-inch-wide fabrics for all decorating purposes (includ-ing upholstery).

Some decorating fabrics are found on a table or shelf and not on rolls. These are called "flat folds." They are usually upholstery-weight fabrics that come from the ends of production runs. These fabrics are usually less expensive, they are available in limited quantities, and you have to guess at the fiber content. But you never know how your luck is on any given day and you might find just what you are looking for.

Regardless of what type of fabric store you shop at, the fabrics are usually displayed together in coordinated collections or grouped by similar colors. This makes it super easy to coordinate fabrics for a room.

Plan Your Attack – What to Expect to Find in a Fabric Store

Fabric stores not only carry fabric, but they carry wonderful notions and tools that make sewing easier. Most stores have what is referred to as a "notion wall." This is where you can find general

Always use a good quality name brand thread for your projects.

sewing notions such as pins, needles, bobbins, grommets, pincushions, tape measures, and so on. Refer to chapter 5 (page 23) to review recom-mended notions specific for home dec sewing.

In the home décor department, you may find additional tools and specialty items that are specific for creating home decorating projects. These may include curtain rods, drapery rings and clips, staple guns, and hemming tools, to name a few. Beautiful trims are also in the decorator department. These products can be incorporated into your project for added impact. Items like pillow forms and batting are usually grouped together in yet another section of the store.

You'll find thread in a large floor display. Don't be confused by all of the types of thread available. Look for "all-purpose thread." This is the type of thread that is used in the projects in this book.

Fabrics 101

In truth, any fabric can be used for a decorating project. However, until you become more accom-plished at sewing, I strongly recommend that you start with woven fabrics (either 45 inches or 54 inches wide) and stay away from sheers and knits. These fabrics are in your not-too-distant future, but avoid them for your first few projects.

Decorative trims can be added to many home decorating projects for texture and additional color.

PART 1
PLAN IT!

Shop for Fabric Like a Pro (Even if You Are Scared Silly)

I can spend hours in a fabric store whether I am working on an actual project or just dreaming of future possibilities. I know my way around my local fabric store as well as I do my home. However, when I explore a new fabric store I am like a kid in a candy store! Here are some of my favorite hints on shopping for fabric.

- To get an idea of how a fabric store is organized and what types of fabric they offer, visit it just for fun, with no intention of buying.

- Touching fabric is important. If the fabric feels too heavy or too light for what you are making, it probably is. Listen to your inner voice. You may seek assurance from a knowledgeable salesperson that works in the store, but I suggest you rely on your instincts.

- "Audition" a potential fabric by unrolling a portion from the bolt or tube. You'll be surprised at how different the color and design looks compared to a small section showing.

- Take your tape measure with you to measure fabric repeats on 54-inch-wide fabric. Large repeats can be a budget buster because of the additional fabric you need to purchase. A tape measure is a "More Splash Than Cash"® reality check.

- Unroll several yards of fabric and bring the selvages together to see if the fabric lies flat without ripples and the designs match exactly at the selvage. If they match, do a little victory dance! This means the design is printed "on grain" and the fabric is ready to sew. If the designs are slightly off at the selvage (1 inch or less) the fabric can still be used with a little manipulation. However, if the designs are off more than 1 inch, seriously consider using another fabric because this fabric will be challenging to work with.

- If you have to match something that already exists in the room, bring the item to the fabric store if possible. If that is not possible, ask to "check out" the fabric overnight so you can see it with what you are trying to match. And if that is not an option, purchase at least a half yard and take it home. Swatches are good for carrying in your purse but not to make a decision on many yards of fabric. The larger the piece of fabric, the easier it is to see how it really works in the room.

Craft and quilt fabrics are folded in half and rolled around cardboard bolts.

Decorator fabrics are displayed on long tubes.

Bolt Notes

Fabrics are usually found on bolts or long tubes. Craft fabrics are usually folded in half lengthwise and rolled onto a bolt. Decorator fabrics are usually rolled on long tubes to avoid creases and wrinkles. You can see the entire width of fabric, which makes it easier to plan your decorating project. The bolt end or a hangtag attached to the tube contains information such as fiber content, width, manufacturer's name, and possibly care instructions.

HOME DEC BECK SAYS:

"It's fun and creative to explore possibilities outside of traditional fabric stores for fabric for your project. Consider refashioning a premade bedspread or a sari into fabulous new accessories."

Look through hanging samples for even more fabric choices.

A store can only display a limited amount of fabric. However, many fabric stores have more samples of fabric that can be special ordered.

Help Is Only a Question Away

Most people who work in a fabric store like to sew and are willing to help you. Don't be afraid to ask for help. The more information you have with you (measurements, color scheme, planned project, etc.), the easier it will be for you to get exactly what you want.

After making your fabric selections take your fabric to the cutting area to get the yardage amount you need.

All fabrics are cut at a designated cutting area on a large cutting table (unless you are purchasing a remnant). A remnant (or flat fold) is a left over portion of fabric that is often offered at a discount price. Remnants are usually found in a separate place in the store. Usually, the pieces are from the end of the bolt, but they can also be pieces with slight flaws. The fabric has been premeasured and priced, and you usually have to buy the entire amount. If that is the case, you can take it directly to the register without stopping at the cutting table.

When you decide what fabric you want, take it to the cutting area. Fabric is sold by the yard or meter, depending on where you live. You can request a portion of a yard so you only have to buy what you need. As the salesperson is taking fabric off of the bolt or tube, look for any flaws in the fabric. If you see a section of the fabric that does not look right, do not hesitate to ask the salesperson to work around it.

Return policies at fabric stores differ so make sure to check their policy. It's best to be confident with your selection before having the fabric cut. Many times stores offer swatches of fabric that you can take home with you. But please don't cut swatches yourself. A salesperson will be happy to do that for you.

Internet Shopping

You can also purchase a wide variety of fabrics online. Many of these sites offer a swatch service. That is, for a small fee, the company will send you swatches of the fabrics you are considering. I *strongly* recommend that you do this so you can touch the fabric and match it to the other items you are using in the room.

Regardless of where you buy your fabric, remember that fabrics are dyed in batches or lots that may differ slightly. If you need a large quantity of fabric for your projects, purchase all the fabric from the same tube to be assured it will match exactly. If more than one tube is needed, make sure they are dyed from the same batch (retailers are accustomed to this request).

PART 2: Stitch It!

Why learn to sew to decorate your home? The cost savings alone can be reason enough! But when you create your own home furnishings, you are not limited to the colors and styles of mass-produced ready-made items that you (and everyone else) can buy. You can make beautiful one-of-a-kind items that reflect your own unique decorating style. "I don't know how to sew!" is not an excuse you can hide behind anymore because this section explains in explicit detail what you need to know to sew all of the projects in this book.

TABLE OF CONTENTS:

Worth Noting

This information is just too important not to mention. Add these tips to your knowledge bank!

Sharp Enough?

Here's a good at-home test to determine if the scissors you have in your drawer are sharp enough to use for sewing.

- Draw a star about the size of a dime on sheer fabric.

- Carefully cut the star from the fabric.

- If the star edges are clean, the scissors are sharp enough. If the edges are jagged, it's time for sharpening or a new pair.

Staying Sharp

Good scissors are important to stress-free sewing. Here are some hints on keeping this invaluable tool ready for action.

- Keep your scissors in the sheath or other protective covering they came in. This will protect the tips from becoming damaged.

- Keep your scissors clean and store them in a cool, dry place. Wipe the blades with a light coating of sewing machine oil and a soft cloth to prevent rust or corrosion (especially if you live in a high-humidity area).

- Try not to drop your scissors because they can be knocked out of alignment, which will affect their cutting ability.

Questions to Ask Yourself When Buying Scissors

All the answers should be yes.

- Are they comfortable in your hand?

- Do they open and close easily?

- When fabric is cut, is the cut edge of the fabric clean?

- Do they easily cut multiple layers?

- Do they cut to the tip of the scissors?

- Is it a name brand?

Hints of Glam

You've found a fabric that you absolutely love, but it is just too expensive. So, what's a girl to do? Don't despair — here are some budget-savvy solutions! Consider these as you plan your projects in this book.

- Use the "to-die-for" fabric as a pillow front and use a less expensive yet coordinating fabric on the back. Make sure the weight of the fabrics are the same.

- Feature the must-have fabric in the center of a set of place mats. Create a "frame" from a contrasting fabric.

- Create your own fabric by stitching small portions of the expensive fabric with other fabrics (like patchwork) that are more in your price range. This solution will work especially well for pillow fronts, table runners, and valances.

- Simple, yet stylish valances can be made from flat panels. Depending on the width of your window, you may be able to use a yard or less.

- Trim the vertical leading edges (the center opening) of a pair of panel curtains with a band of the expensive fabric.

- Recover a small ottoman or footstool to make a decorating statement with the fabric you can't do without.

- Approximately 1 yard of 54-inch-wide fabric will recover four average-size dining room chair seats.

HOME DEC BECK SAYS:

"If I'm being creative, you can't expect me
   to be neat too!"

5 | Make It Work!

**An efficient
work area and
the right tools
will make sewing
a pleasurable
experience.**

B efore diving into your sewing project, spend some time planning your work area (even if it is temporary) and gathering the tools you'll need. An efficient work area and the right tools will make the entire process a more pleasurable experience. Try to incorporate as many of the suggestions in this chapter as possible.

Set the Scene

Ideally, set up a permanent work area for the duration of a project. Time and momentum are lost when you have to break down your work area after you finish each day.

- Use a clean, sturdy table (a dining or kitchen table is perfect!) to use as your cutting and sewing table. A wobbly card table is not the best choice, but it will work if nothing else is available to you.

- Make your work surface as large as possible. If you're using the dining room table, extend the table to its maximum size. You should have at least 6 inches on each side of the sewing machine for some "elbow room."

- Large, inexpensive, and portable cardboard cutting surfaces (40 inches by 72 inches) are available in fabric stores and make great temporary work surfaces. Of course, if all else fails, move the furniture and use the floor!

- Set up a pressing station near your sewing station. To save time when sewing, arrange your ironing board at a right angle to and at the same height as your sewing table. This way you can just sew, turn, press, turn, and continue sewing — without leaving your chair. How handy is that?

- Have plenty of light at your workspace. Sewing in a too-dark space will contribute to eye fatigue. Consider adding a desk lamp to your sewing table.

- Keep a small wastebasket beside your sewing machine to catch trimmed threads and snippets of fabric.

Store More

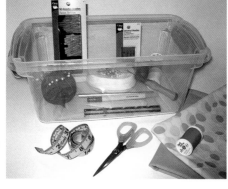

Keep your tools together in a container. A toolbox, a cute lunchbox, a tackle box, or a bucket are some alternative ideas for your sewing basket.

- Clear, resealable bags are a great (and inexpensive) way to keep your sewing basket organized. Use them to keep together bobbins, spools of thread, safety pins, buttons, and trims.

- Inexpensive shoe organizers hung on the back of a door have lots of pockets to hold all kinds of stuff. You can see everything at a glance if you get one made of transparent plastic. This is a perfect storage solution if you live in tight quarters.

- Plastic containers are a neat and handy way to store your project between sewing sessions.

Take a Seat!

You are going to be sitting at the sewing machine for stretches of time. You need to be as comfortable as possible.

- A good office chair is great for sewing. Sewing can be tough on the back so be sure your chair is comfortable. When sitting, your knees should be slightly lower than your hips. You should be able to reach the foot pedal on the floor without stretching your legs.

- Position your chair so it is squarely in front of the sewing machine. Your hands, wrists, and forearms should be level with the sewing machine bed.

Tooling Around – Essential Tools for Your Home Dec Sewing Kit

These are the "must have" tools. You can find all of these in the fabric store.

- Dressmaker shears (8- to 10-inch blade length)

- Embroidery scissors (less than 4 inches long)

- Pinking shears

- Seam ripper

- Liquid seam sealant

- All-purpose nickel-plated steel straight pins with large, round heads ($1^1/_2$ to $1^7/_8$ inches long)

- Universal machine needles in assorted sizes (especially sizes 80/12 and 90/14)

- Handsewing needles in assorted sizes (a package that includes sizes 5-10)

- Pincushion or magnetic pin holder

- All-purpose thread

- Iron and a sturdy ironing surface

- Press cloth

- Iron cleaner

- Spray bottle

- Point turner

- Retractable metal tape measure

- Transparent ruler (6 inches by 24 inches is the most versatile size)

- Yardstick

- Flexible tape measure (with a length of at least 120 inches)

- Seam gauge

- Drapery hem gauge

- Assortment of fabric markers (chalk and air or water soluble)

- Paper-backed fusible tape

- Extra bobbins

Grab Your Gear and Sew!

Once you have your work area set up, it's time to gather the tools you'll need. Specific tools for sewing are what make the difference between your project going well—or not!

A Cut Above

You hear the word "scissors" used more often than you hear the word "shears" even though they are different tools used for different purposes in the sewing world. You can easily tell them apart because scissors are smaller and have two round holes for the fingers. Shears have a round hole for the thumb and a larger oval for two or three fingers. The importance of good sewing shears will not be evident until you start sewing. You will quickly realize how much easier it is to use a pair of shears because they cut fabric like they are going through butter instead of a tough piece of meat. I have a pair of shears that are designated only for fabric and I protect them like a lion protects her newborn cub (cutting paper destroys the sharp edge). In fact, I have a note taped to them that warns any unsuspecting soul "You Touch, You Die!"

Bent-handled Dressmaker Shears

Shears with blade lengths of 8 to 10 inches are recom-
mended. Get what feels most comfortable for you. Right- and left-handed models are available. You should not feel any resistance when the blades are being opened and closed; they should operate smoothly.

Embroidery Scissors

These scissors have narrow sharply pointed blades (about 4 inches long). Keep them next to your machine and grab them to clip unsightly threads.

Pinking Shears

The unique feature with these shears is the zigzag blades. They cut fabric in a zigzag pattern instead of a straight line. These zigzagged edges keep the fabric from fraying and are used primarily on seam allowances as a seam finish.

Seam Ripper

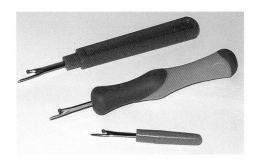

This tool is designed to remove any misplaced stitches. A seam ripper has a sharp point that slides under the stitches and cuts the thread without harming the fabric.

Rotary Cutter and Mat

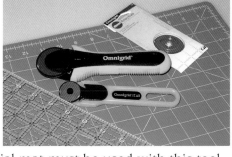

The rotary cutter looks like a pizza cutter and can be used by left-handed or right-handed sewers. A special mat must be used with this tool to protect cutting surfaces and also preserve the sharpness of the rotary cutting blade.

Quilters use these tools when cutting strips and small pieces of cotton fabric. I find the rotary cutting system impractical for most home decorating projects and do not recommend it when cutting 54-inch-wide decorator fabric. The special cutting boards are not made large enough, and you have to pay particular attention to the way the design is printed on the fabric. However, if you are comfortable with the tools, you can use them for the smaller projects in this book. Always use extreme caution with these tools.

Liquid Seam Sealant

This colorless liquid prevents fabric or seams from fraying or raveling. The sealant dries clear and withstands many washings.

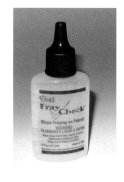

On Pins and Needles

Small, but mightily important in the overall sewing scheme, pins and needles can't be forgotten when putting together your decorating sewing kit.

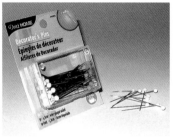

Pins

Straight pins act as a third hand – they hold two pieces of fabric together so you can focus on what you are doing.

- Choose nickel-plated steel straight pins, $1^1/_2$ to $1^7/_8$ inches long.

- Large "heads" are easier to grasp and won't hide in the carpet if dropped on the floor.

- Buy a brand name pin (found on the notions wall). Never buy pins from the bargain bin. They are simply not durable enough and will bend easily. Bargain pins are a nightmare.

- Pitch any bent, nicked, or rusted pins.

- Keep your pins handy by inserting them in a pincushion or magnetic pin holder.

Machine Needles

This one little item has a big job to do — it single-handedly determines how well your machine makes a stitch.

- "Universal" needles are fine for most fabrics.

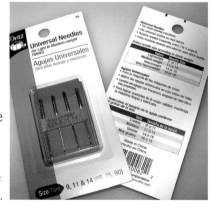

- Needles are assigned numbers that relate to their size. In general, the lighter weight the fabric, the smaller the needle needed.

- For most decorating projects, choose size 80/12 or size 90/14.

- Needles wear out and need to be replaced regularly. A good habit to develop is to always start a new project with a new needle.

- The needle packet will indicate the type of fabric the needles are appropriate for.

Handsewing Needles

Yes, you may have to do a little handsewing. So, just in case, choose a pack of assorted sizes that includes sizes 5 through 10 (the higher the number, the thinner the needle).

Pincushion and Magnetic Pin Holder

These must-have gadgets are handy places to store pins. You can't go wrong with the traditional tomato cushion and emery-filled strawberry (used to sharpen your needles). But also consider the magnetic pin holders. These are especially handy to sweep pins off the floor.

Thread Head

You simply can't sew without thread. This important component is what holds everything together. In the fabric store, thread is organized first by type and then by color.

- All-purpose thread is perfect for the projects in this book. You'll also need carpet or waxed button thread to sew buttons on your home decorating items.

- Avoid bargain-bin threads at all cost! They are much lower in quality and strength to name brands; they throw off excessive lint, knot quickly, and break easily because of the inferior fibers used to manufacture them. The pennies you save are simply not worth the headaches inferior thread can cause.

- Thread color should be one shade darker than the main color in your fabric (it appears lighter when stitched).

Pressing Issues

When sewing, an iron is your best offense to preventing unsightly wrinkles in your project. The secret is to press as you sew, and then when you're done, you're done.

Iron

Choose an iron that allows you to control the amount of steam (from no steam to a heavy burst of steam).

A vertical steam feature is handy for keeping window treatments neat and tidy. Some manufacturers offer a safety feature that automatically turns the iron off if it's not used for a period of time. Some people like this feature, others (me included) find it annoying.

Ironing Surface

A firmly padded, sturdy, cotton-covered ironing surface is a must. A standard ironing board is nice for smaller projects, but can be challenging to use for larger projects such as floor-length window treatments or a duvet cover. A large, portable pressing pad is a good alternative for larger projects. They are also easy to store.

Press Cloth

A loosely woven 100 percent white cotton cloth helps to prevent shine or even burn marks when pressing fabric. It goes between the hot iron and the fabric.

Iron Cleaner

Keep your iron surface clean and shiny. If you've ever scorched something or melted a fusible on your iron soleplate (we've all done it), you'll notice a dingy, sticky coating that prevents your iron from gliding easily. To remedy this, use a special iron cleaning cream on a regular basis.

Spray Bottle

Plastic spray bottles are inexpensive (I got mine at the drugstore) but really handy to help remove wrinkles, especially from cotton fabrics. On the wrong side, lightly spray a coating of water on the fabric before applying the heat of an iron (or you can spray the press cloth instead). The combination of the water and the heat produces steam that helps press out creases. Always try this technique on fabric scraps because the water may stain some fabrics.

Turning the Corner

Sharp corners on a pillow or duvet cover are outward signs of a job well done. No matter how carefully you sew, this special tool comes in handy to make sure your corners are the best they can be.

Point Turner

This unassuming and inexpensive tool has a pointed end used for creating sharp

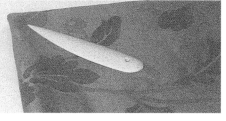

corners in items such as pillows. The round end is good for creating smooth curves. This is my favorite and most used tool.

For Good Measure

The axiom "Measure twice, cut once" is aptly applied to any and all sewing projects.

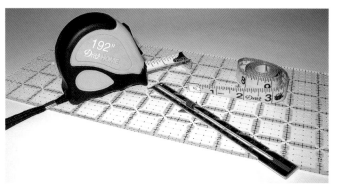

Retractable Metal Tape Measure

A retractable tape measure is a must when taking measurements for walls, windows, and more.

Transparent Ruler

A 6-inch-by-24-inch ruler is the most versatile type of transparent tool. Typically, this tool is used for quilt making, but it is invaluable for many home decorating projects. The ruler has a 1-inch grid printed on the surface for quick reference and to help you measure accurately.

Flexible Tape Measure

This tool is very flexible – perfect for measuring the size of a pillow form, the perimeter of a cushion. Get one that has numbers printed on both sides and is at least 120 inches long.

Seam Gauge

A seam gauge is a 6-inch ruler that has a double-pointed, movable slide that stays in place at a selected measurement. This handy tool helps make accurate measurements quickly. Despite its name, it can be used for more purposes than measuring seam allowances.

Drapery Hem Gauge

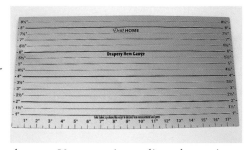

This extra-wide measuring tool makes measuring and pressing hems quick and easy. You can iron directly on it.

On the Mark

The secret to successful sewing is accurate measuring and marking. Use specially designed fabric markers to mark your fabric temporarily. Here's a sample of a few.

Water Soluble Fabric Marker

This is a felt-tip marker usually with blue ink, and is good to use on light-colored fabrics. It disappears when water is applied to the mark. Always test the marker on the fabric you are using. Sometimes a chemical reaction occurs between the marker and special fabric finishes and the marks can't be removed regardless of how much water is applied. Do not apply heat to any temporary marks because the heat could make them permanent.

Air Soluble Marker

Similar to a water soluble fabric marker, this marker contains purple ink. The marks made on fabric with this marker will disappear automatically within a short period of time (it varies by manufacturer). This marker is not as effective in areas that are humid because the marks will disappear quickly. Always test this marker on the fabric you are using to make sure it disappears.

Dressmaker's Chalk

This type of marker is good for dark fabrics. The marks may fade over time, or you can easily brush them away.

Marking Pencil

This marker shows up well on dark fabrics. It's available in many different colors. The marks can be removed with a drop of water, they will fade over time, or they can be simply brushed off.

Paper-backed Fusible Tape

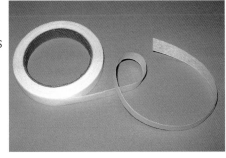

This tape comes on a roll and in various widths and is used to hold two pieces of fabric together. One side of the tape has a coating of glue or adhesive that is activated when heat is applied. The paper backing protects your iron from being gummed up with the adhesive. Some of these tapes can permanently bond fabrics together and substitute for sewing a seam (think "no-sew"). However, for the projects in this book, select a tape that can be stitched through. Read the manufacturer's label carefully to make sure you select the type you can stitch through.

Project-Specific Tools and Supplies

At one time or another, you will need a specialty item to complete your project. These items are more "project specific" than those recommended for your decorating sewing kit. The following items are needed for various projects in this book.

Cover Button Forms and Frames

Kits are available to make round or square covered buttons in your choice of fabrics. Decorative frames are also available to give your project even more style.

Grommets

These plastic rings are inserted through fabrics so a curtain rod can be woven through or hooks can be attached.

Batting

Batting is primarily used as the middle layer in quilts to provide warmth and

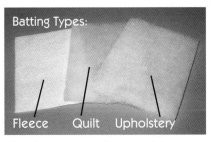

dimension when quilted. But it is also used in home decorating projects for many different purposes. Batting is available in prepackaged amounts or sold by the yard. It comes in many types. Fleece type batting is very dense in appearance where as regular quilt batting is more loosely constructed. Batting used for upholstering is much thicker than quilt batting and is sold by the yard. It usually comes on a huge roll; ask a store employee for help.

Loose Fiberfill

This filling material is fluffy in appearance. It is an alternative product used to stuff pillows. It's always handy to have a bag around your sewing room in case you have a creative moment and no pillow forms!

HOME DEC BECK SAYS:

"Wind several bobbins before you start a project; you will always have a spare at your fingertips. keep the filled bobbins together (and keep the threads from dangling) in a foam toe separator, the kind used for pedicures."

Pillow Forms

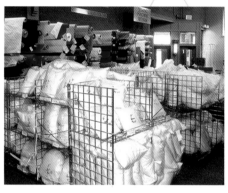

Pillow forms are prestuffed shapes that are inserted into pillow covers. These forms are generously stuffed with loose polyester fiberfill. Some-times, I remove some of the stuffing because they are too "fat" for the project I am making. More expensive and luxurious pillow forms are stuffed with down. Pillow forms are available in a variety of sizes and shapes.

Fusible Interfacing

This fabric stiffener adds structure and stability to fabrics. It comes in different weights that provide different stability. Interfacing is available with or without a fusible backing. A fusible interfacing has little beads of glue on one side that is activated when heat is applied. It is ironed to the wrong side of fabrics in some projects.

Twill Tape

This washable tape is used to make sturdy ties in the duvet cover.

Shade Cord

This firm, smooth nylon cord is used to rig Roman shades and other drawn-up window treat-ments.

Individual Roman Shade Rings

These plastic rings are used to construct Roman shades. The rings act as guides on the back of the shade for the cord to operate the shade smoothly.

Screw Eyes

These metal screws have an enclosed circle on one end. They are inserted into mounting boards to guide Roman shade cords across the width of the window.

Cord Pull

Loose ends of shade cords are inserted into this decorative device to help keep cords orderly on a Roman shade.

Cord Cleat

Attach this cleat to the wall or window frame to hold Roman shades at a particular height. The shade cords are wrapped around the cleat in a figure-eight configuration to secure them.

Awl

This sharp-pointed tool is used to start holes for small wood screws and screw eyes.

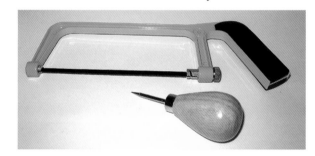

Minisaw

This cutting tool is used to cut mounting boards for window treatments.

Where to Shop

Most of the other items in this chapter can be found at a fabric store, but you'll need to venture into other stores, such as an art supply store or a home improvement store to complete some of the projects in this book.

Clockwise: Cord Cleat, Screw Eyes, Shade Cord, Cord Pull, Individual Rings. ◄

6 | *Meet Your New Best Friend*

Of all your sewing tools, a sewing machine is the most important.

Since you are going to be attached to your sewing machine, you might as well like it (him? her?). And, I promise — you will like it so much more if you know how it operates.

Of all your sewing tools, a sewing machine is probably the largest financial investment you will make. Doing your research before you buy a machine will help you make a confident purchase.

All sewing machine manufacturers make good machines. The adage "you get what you pay for" is very true when purchasing a sewing machine. My advice is to buy the best machine you can afford. An honest evaluation of your sewing needs and goals will help you resist an overeager salesperson's enthusiasm so you don't end up with an overpriced dust catcher.

In the Making

Whether you have a brand new machine or are using a hand-me-down, make sure you know how to

- Identify the parts of the machine (see the separate list and diagram that follows)

- Turn the machine on and off

- Thread the machine

- Wind the bobbin and place it correctly in the machine

- Remove, replace, and thread the needle

- Adjust the thread tension

- Change the stitch length

- Adjust the needle position

- Select stitch patterns (such as straight stitch, zigzag, hem stitch)

- Reverse stitch

- Operate the handwheel

- Control the speed of the machine with the foot pedal

- Lift/lower the presser foot

Parts to Play

Take a good look at your machine and compare it to the diagram provided. If you have your manual, open it to the pages that show where these parts are on your machine. Even though every brand of sewing machine has unique features, they all contain the same basic components. They might be at different places and look slightly different than what is shown, but believe me, they are there! Identify them on your machine.

Parts Description

1. Reverse Stitch: At the beginning and end of most seams, you need to take a few stitches in reverse to ensure the seam doesn't come undone.

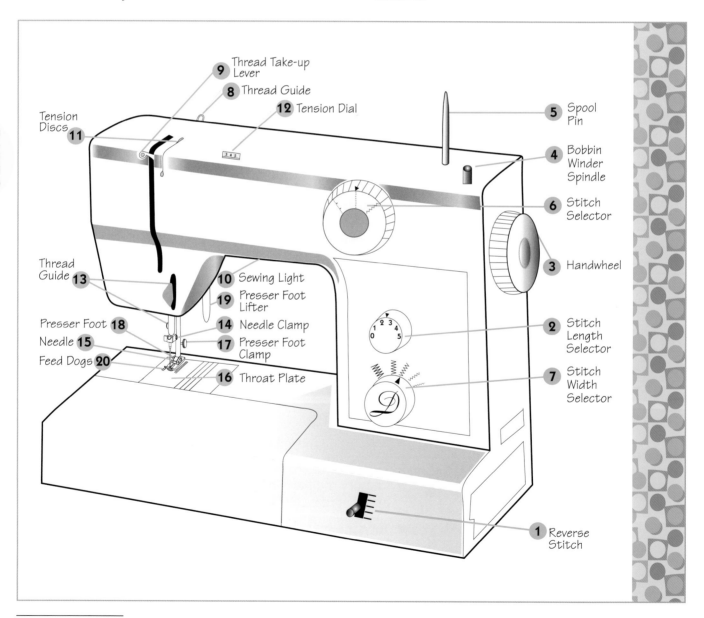

2. Stitch Length Selector: With slight adjustments, you can change the stitch size. The smaller the stitch, the harder it is to remove if you make a mistake. The longest stitch is only meant to be temporary and is sometimes called a basting stitch.

3. Handwheel: This wheel makes a complete rotation with every stitch. You can move the handwheel manually by turning it toward you. As the handwheel is turned, the needle goes up and down. Do not turn the handwheel away from you. However, a little jiggle every now and then will help you if the needle gets stuck in the fabric.

4. Bobbin Winder Spindle: This pin holds the bobbin while the thread winds from the spool onto the bobbin.

5. Spool Pin: Holds the spool of thread for sewing and winding the bobbin.

6. Stitch Selector: Determines what type of stitch the machine stitches. From a straight stitch, a zigzag stitch, a hem stitch, a buttonhole stitch or a decorative stitch.

7. Stitch Width Selector: With a simple adjustment, this gauge determines how wide the zigzag and hemstitch stitches are.

8. Thread Guides: These features hold and guide the thread as it goes from the spool to the needle.

9. Thread Take-Up Lever: This lever is on the front of the machine and moves up and down in sync with the needle as a stitch is created. When the take-up lever is in the highest position, a stitch is complete and the needle is out of the fabric. Always finish stitching with the take-up lever in its highest position, even if you have to move the handwheel (toward you) by hand to accomplish this.

10. Sewing Light: This light highlights the stitching area. It comes on when the power is turned on.

11. Tension Disc: The looks of this mechanism vary the most from sewing machine to sewing

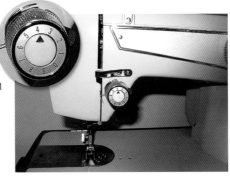

machine, but they all regulate the tension that is applied to the top thread.

12. Tension Dial: This knob or dial controls the tension of the top thread.

13. Thread Guide: These guides literally guide the thread as it goes from the spool to the needle.

14. Needle Clamp: This clamp holds the needle in place.

15. Needle: This small, slender object with a sharp point at one end has an eye, or hole, where the thread goes through.

16. Throat Plate: Located under the needle, this metal piece has a hole in it where the needle goes down and the bobbin thread comes up. It has etched guidelines or markings to help you determine and keep a straight and even seam width.

17. Presser Foot Clamp: This screw or clamp is used to remove and attach different presser feet. Some machines have feet that just snap on.

18. Presser Foot: This is lowered before stitching and it holds two fabrics in place. There are many feet available for different sewing tasks. Check your manual to see what presser feet came with your machine.

19. Presser Foot Lifter: This lever raises and lowers the presser foot. Do this gently. Don't let the presser foot slam down onto the feed dogs.

20. Feed Dogs: Located under the throat plate, this teethlike mechanism holds the fabric against the presser foot as the machine stitches and also moves back and forth to feed the fabric under the needle.

PART 2
STITCH IT!

Sewing Machine Checklist

The checklist on page 35 is a list of some sewing machine features to consider if you are purchasing a sewing machine. These features are not found on all machines, or they function differently from brand to brand. You may or may not find them useful for your sewing needs. Ask the dealer to demonstrate the features. Indicate if the feature is important to you by placing a check in the box in front of the feature. Take this with you as you shop for your sewing machine. A printable version can be found on my website.

▶ www.MoreSplashThanCash.com

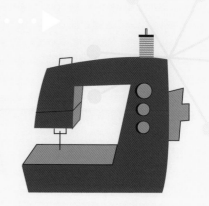

21. Bobbin/Bobbin Case: The bobbin holds the lower thread. It is placed in a bobbin case that controls the tension of the bobbin thread.

22. Foot Pedal: This is the "gas pedal" of the sewing machine. Press on it to make the machine operate. The pressure you apply controls the speed.

Where to Buy a Sewing Machine

You can buy a sewing machine in many places—from sewing machine stores to yard sales. Here are several places to buy a machine and their pros and cons.

Sewing Machine Dealers

Many sewing machine dealers sell more than one brand of sewing machine. If you have a specific brand in mind, start by looking for a dealer that carries that brand. Sewing machine dealers are very knowledgeable about the brands of machines they carry. They also offer advice, troubleshooting, parts, factory-authorized repair service, notions, specialty items, classes, and sewing clubs. In short, they support the products they sell.

Advantages of Buying from a Local Sewing Machine Dealer

Sewing machine dealers specialize in selling sewing machines. They attend conventions and

conferences to learn about the product they sell. Consider the following advantages:

- Help is a phone call away if you experience a malfunction with the sewing machine. Dealers have direct support from the machine's manufacturer so any problem can be solved easily.

- Most dealers are trained to repair the brand of sewing machine they sell and repair the machines on site and in a timely manner.

- Classes are many times included with a machine purchase from a dealer. This gives you an opportunity to learn everything about your machine and about any optional equipment that may interest you.

- Many dealers will take back the machines they sell as trade-ins. This will give you an opportunity to upgrade your machine at a later time.

Discount Retailers and Chain Stores

The sales support you receive from discount retailers and chain stores is minimal. They usually have a small selection, and you probably won't receive any advice from them in regard to the operation and maintenance of your machine. The employees are not trained about the machines they carry, and the stores seldom offer classes. You might save a few dollars, but will it be worth it in the long run?

Mass Merchandiser

Many large retailers (such as Sears) sell branded machines. Since the machines have the store's brand on them, they appear to be made by that company but in reality, another manufacturer

PART 2
STITCH IT!

WOULD LIKE THIS FEATURE	Feature	Description of Features	Points to Consider
	Accessory Storage Area	Small compartments	• store small tools and notions that you use all of the time
	Adjustable Feed Dog	Drops the toothy mechanism below the sewing surface	• can do freehand work • keeps from damaging sheer fabrics
	Adjustable Presser Foot	Regulates how tightly the machine holds fabric while sewing	• prevents puckering in fine fabrics • ensures that knits don't stretch out of shape
	Automatic Bobbin Fill Stop	Automatically stops the bobbin winding process when the sensor tells it that the bobbin is full	• overfilled bobbins can cause tension problems.
	Automatic Needle Stop, Up/Down	Directs the machine to stop stitching with the needle always in either the raised or lowered position	• if stopped in the up position you can remove the fabric from under the needle effortlessly • when stopped in the down position, the fabric can be easily pivoted when stitching corners
	Automatic Tension Adjustment	Helps avoid loopy stitches for the upper thread	• loopy stitches can jam the machine or bend the needle
	Bobbin Loading Position	Location on the machine where the bobbin is inserted	• choose from either a top or front load; both types are efficient
	Bobbin Winder	Winds thread onto bobbin	• different positions and steps can be used to accomplish this • thread should wind around bobbin evenly
	Built-in Stitches	The embroidery or decorative stitches featured on the machine without any additional accessories needed	• straight, zigzag, and blind hem stitches are a must • decorative stitches can be used to embellish your project
	Buttonholer	Makes stylized machine buttonholes	• one-step process is easier and more precise than multiple step
	Flat Bed	Removable platform	• provides wider sewing surface on a portable machine • can be removed to reveal a free arm
	Free Arm	A small, narrow working surface	• allows you to slide projects with narrow openings (such as a cuff of a sleeve) under the needle
	Multiple Needle Positions	Allows the needle to be moved from the standard center position to far right, far left, and points in between	• allows for more precise sewing
	Needle Threader	Device that assists in threading the needle	• reduces eyestrain and frustration
	Reverse Stitching Button	When activated, machine stitches backwards	• located in different positions on the machine • some machines stay in reverse position until deactivated; other buttons need to be pressed continuously
	Sewing "Adviser"	Automatically recommends the stitch and presser foot to use for the type of fabric being used	• available on more expensive machines
	Specialized Presser Feet	Designed with specific tasks in mind such as blind hems, buttonholes, cording	• the number and type of feet that are included depends on the brand and model
	Speed Control	Determines the sewing speed	• machine will stitch slower or faster depending on your comfort level
	Tension Setting	Determines the quality of the stitch	• some machines have a sensor that automatically sets the tension to the type of fabric being stitched; others can be manually adjusted
	Thread Cutter	Cuts the top and bobbin thread automatically after stitching a seam	• others have a blade in a convenient location to cut the threads in the same step as you remove the fabric from under the needle

PART 2
STITCH IT!

makes them and places the store brand on the product. These machines are usually sold in sealed boxes and often at a lower price. You are completely on your own when purchasing a machine from such a source because no classes or product support is available.

Mail Order/Internet

This is another way to purchase a sewing machine (you can order one in your jammies). Peruse many options before making a decision. However, clarify the company's return policy, warranty, and service policies before buying. Only do this if you are absolutely certain that you are comfortable with buying a machine without test-driving it first.

Classified Ads, Yard or Garage Sales

Great bargains can be found here. But many times the machine is missing parts, feet, and that all-important manual. See if you can sew with it before you buy.

Buying Your First Machine

Just as you test-drive a car before you buy it, you ought to test-drive a sewing machine. Observe how it sews on a variety of fabrics, how easy it is to change the presser feet, whether you like the different stitches, how it sounds, and how you like the feel of it.

Consider the type of sewing you plan to do. Refer to the list of sewing machine features (page 36) to give you an idea of what features you'd like to have to accomplish your sewing goals. Take this list with you when you shop for a sewing machine. Compare the list of features you would like to the capabilities of the models offered. Keep in mind that the more options you want, the higher the price. Sewing machine prices vary from a hundred dollars to thousands of dollars and it's very easy to be seduced by all of the features.

Take your own thread and fabric to the dealer and ask that they be used for the demonstration and for your test-drive. You are trying to create a sewing experience as true to real life as possible. This is a common and practical request. The experts at the dealers will demonstrate how the machine you are interested in operates. Don't be afraid to ask questions during the demonstration. You are making a significant investment, and you want to be sure you are making an informed

decision. After the demonstration, it is your time to sit and sew. Sewing machine dealers have floor models available for this purpose. Practice threading the machine, winding the bobbin, inserting the bobbin, and, of course, stitching. Plan to spend some time testing out the different models.

If You Are Using a Borrowed or Used Machine

If you just pulled a machine from a closet, out of the alley, or brought it home from a yard sale, you can safely assume it has been sitting untouched for quite a while. Honestly, it will be a minor miracle if it starts, much less stitches without any problems. Just like a car needs regular maintenance to run properly, so does a sewing machine. So before you do anything else, get that machine to a repair shop for a tune-up.

While you are there, inquire about a lesson to learn how to operate your machine. If you have the manual that came with the machine, you are ahead of the game. But sometimes sitting down with someone familiar with operating a machine lessens the learning curve.

Finding Old Manuals

The manual that came with the machine explains all of the features on your machine. However, if you are not lucky enough to have the manual, you can probably find one. A local dealer that carries your brand of sewing machine may be able to help. If the dealers in your area don't carry your brand, try the sewing machine manufacturer's website or sites that specialize in old manuals. Knowing the make and model of your machine will assure that you will receive the correct manual.

PART 2
STITCH IT!

"This chapter is like a boot camp for sewers – only you don't have to leave your home!"

7 | Need-to-Know Info

This chapter is packed full of information to get you on the sewing fast track.

Use the correct bobbin for your machine.

Deactivate the motion of the needle.

Dislodge thread from spool to unwind.

Great news for those of you who already know how to thread your sewing machine, wind the bobbin, and change a needle: you can skip this whole chapter! This chapter is packed full of information you can use as a general reference. For specifics, refer to your owner's manual for your machine. If you can't find or acquire a manual, you will have to learn how to thread your machine by good old trial and error (hopefully, not too many errors). Be fearless! The following information is a general approach to winding the bobbin and threading the machine. Compare the machine in the illustration to yours. There may be some differences, but basically, all machines are threaded the same way.

The Great Windup

The bobbin is a small spool that is wound with thread that ultimately provides the bottom half of a stitch. Bobbins are sized precisely to fit specific brands of sewing machines. Make sure the bobbin you are using is for your make and model. Here's how to wind a bobbin (fill it with thread).

1. Deactivate the up-and-down motion of the needle before winding the bobbin. On many of the newer machines, the needle is automatically deactivated when the bobbin is placed on the bobbin pin and it is engaged. On older machines you may have to deactivate it manually.

2. On one end of the spool there is a little notch that secured the thread onto the spool when the thread was originally wound onto the spool from the manufacturer. Begin unwinding the thread at this notch by dislodging the thread. You will need to unwind the tread several times before you can actually see the thread unwind from

the spool. This invisible space is called the well, and is needed for the manufacturing process.

3. Once the thread has begun to unwind, place the spool of thread on the vertical or horizontal spool pin (usually on the top right side of the machine). If the thread spool has paper labels covering the ends, uncover the holes by poking a hole in the paper.

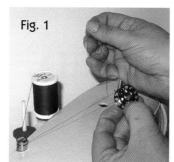
Fig. 1

4. Arrange the thread around the thread guides needed to wind the bobbin. The number of guides will vary with the type or brand of machine. Make sure the thread is secure within the guides (it's like flossing your teeth). Insert the cut end of the thread from inside of the bobbin and up through the hole so the thread comes out through the top (fig 1).

Place spool on spool pin through the thread guide, then through the bobbin.

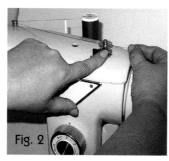
Fig. 2

5. Place the bobbin on the bobbin winding spindle and snap it into place (fig. 2).

Snap bobbin into place.

6. Hold the thread out to the right of the machine and gently press the foot pedal. The thread will begin to wind around the bobbin.

7. Allow the thread to wind around the bobbin a few times. Note: Make sure the needle does not go up and down. Remove your foot from the foot pedal to stop the machine. Then cut the thread you were holding close to the bobbin.

8. Continue to wind the bobbin until it is full. Keep the speed consistent to ensure that the thread is wound evenly onto the bobbin.

9. When the bobbin is completely wound, disengage the bobbin winder and remove the bobbin from the machine. The thread should be wound evenly onto the bobbin and feel firm to the touch. If it is loose, or wound unevenly, unwind it completely and start over. Throw the used thread away.

10. Place the bobbin into the bobbin case; and make sure there is a tail about 8 inches long coming from the bobbin (fig. 3).

Fig. 3

Insert bobbin into the bobbin case.

Fig. 4

11. Filled bobbins are loaded into machines a variety of ways. Check your machine manual to see how to properly insert the bobbin into your machine. Bobbins are loaded into a machine two ways: inserted into a separate bobbin case and then placed in the machine (fig. 4) or dropped into a case below the needle.

Place bobbin case into the bobbin compartment.

How to Thread a Sewing Machine

Some machines make it so easy for you to thread them because they have printed numbers to direct you through the threading path. If yours doesn't have this feature, and you think it will help you, mark them yourself. Your manual will show details of how to thread your machine.

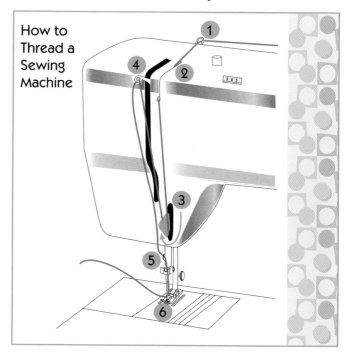
How to Thread a Sewing Machine

NOTE: Make sure the presser foot is up before beginning. Place the spool of thread on either the vertical or horizontal spool pin.

1. Take the thread across the machine and through or around the first thread guide (usually on the top left side of the machine).

2. Pull the thread down vertically through the tension guide. This is where most threading mistakes are made.

3. Make a U-turn and take the thread up and through the next thread guide toward the take-up lever.

4. Insert the thread through the take-up lever (some have an eye; others have a slot). This is part of the machine that moves up and down.

5. Draw the thread down, around, and through any remaining thread guides toward the needle.

6. Thread the needle. Most needles are threaded from front to back but some are threaded from left to right and still others right to left. Check your manual to see how your needle is threaded.

NOTE: Arrange the thread to go between the opening of the presser foot. Pull the thread to the side of the machine several inches.

How to Bring Up the Bobbin Thread

To form a stitch, the bobbin thread needs to come up through the hole in the throat plate.

1. Make sure the machine is threaded correctly (including the needle) and the bobbin is inserted properly. Several inches of bobbin thread should protrude from the bobbin compartment (fig. 5).

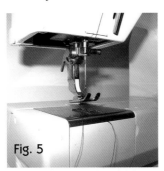
Fig. 5

2. Pull several inches of thread through the needle. Hold the thread in your left hand. With your right hand, gently turn the handwheel toward you until the

Fig. 6

needle goes all the way down and back up. As you do this, the top thread will catch the bobbin thread in the bobbin compartment (fig. 6).

Fig. 7

3. Pull the loose end of the needle thread; you should see a loop of thread under the presser foot (fig. 7).

4. Pull the loop all the way out from under the presser foot until you have two loose ends of thread (fig. 8).

Fig. 8

Fig. 9

5. Place both the needle and bobbin threads under the presser foot and take them back off the machine bed (fig. 9).

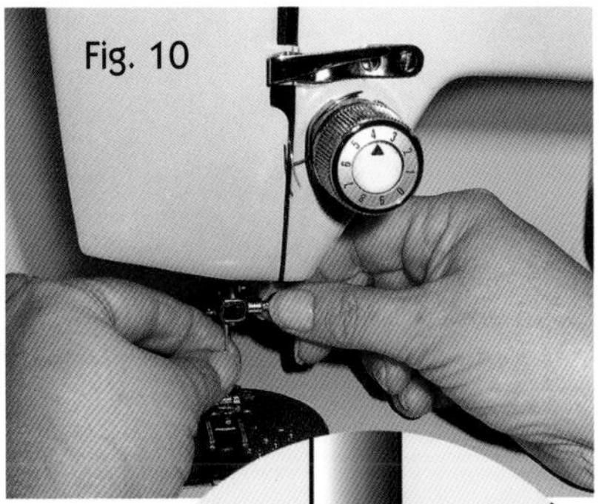

How to Change the Needle

This is the most universal way to change a needle.

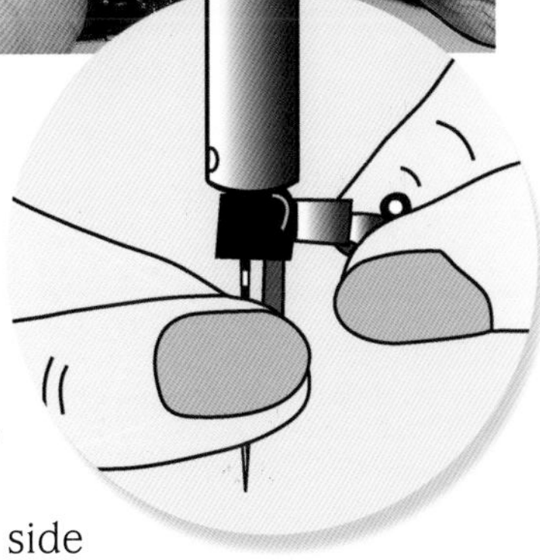

1. Turn the machine off.

Fig. 10

2. Loosen the needle screw or clamp (fig. 10). Remember, "Righty tighty, lefty loosey."

3. Gently slide the needle out. Make note of where the needle's flat side is positioned as it is removed (usually the flat side of the shank faces away from you).

4. Throw the old needle away immediately!

5. Orient the new needle the same way it was removed. Slide the needle up into the channel as far as it goes. Then tighten the screw or needle clamp to hold it in place.

Test Stitch

If the machine is not threaded correctly (or another problem exists), the stitch quality will reveal it. In a perfect stitch, the threads are pulled into the stitch with equal tension and the stitches look exactly the same on both sides of the fabric, without any puckering in the fabric (fig. 11).

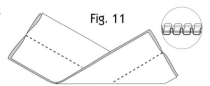

Fig. 11

Since every machine has a certain threading sequence, it only takes one missed step to cause stitch problems. If the stitches on your test are not good, do not panic! The first thing to do, always, is to check the needle. It may not be inserted correctly, it might be bent, or it might be the wrong needle for the fabric (check the label on the needle case to be sure). If that doesn't solve the problem, unthread the machine completely (removing the bobbin too) and rethread the machine from the beginning. If these simple actions don't correct the problem, you may have to investigate further to find what needs to be adjusted. There are more solutions to stitch problems in chapter 11, "HELP!" (Help for Every Little Problem).

Avoid Tension Headaches

Fig. 12

Most machines work great if the tension setting is between 3 and 5 (fig 12). If your machine just came from the dealer (because you purchased it new or it just had a tune-up), the tension is already set. However, as you use different fabrics, stitches, and thread, the tension may need to be adjusted slightly to accommodate their unique characteristics. Symptoms of tension imbalance include stitches with loops on the front or back, thread pulls when turning a corner, or thread that breaks while stitching. If you have determined the tension needs adjusting (after changing the needle and rethreading the machine), refer to chapter 11, "HELP!" for instructions.

You've Got That Loving Feeling!

If you "show the love" to your sewing machine, it will love you in return. It will stitch its little heart out for you in perfect harmony every time you make a project. But there's a catch: you have to take care of it. The following maintenance steps will keep your machine happy if you do them on a regular basis.

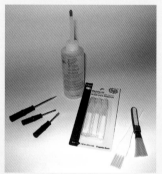

Cleaning tools for your sewing machine.

- Wipe any dust that has accumulated on the outer surface of the machine.

- Use a soft brush to remove any lint that has collected in the small crevices.

- Open the throat plate and clean out the bobbin compartment. This area is susceptible to collecting a major amount of lint.

- Use tweezers to remove pieces of thread or lint that can't be brushed away.

- Add oil to the motor to keep the motor purring like a kitten. Your manual will show you when, where, and how much to oil your machine. Note: Some machines are self-lubricating and don't need to be oiled. Be sure to check with the manual or your dealer before proceeding.

- Get a tune-up from a professional every year.

HOME DEC BECK SAYS:

"If I stitch fast enough, does it count as an aerobic exercise?"

8 | Itchin' To Stitch

Only three basic sewing techniques are used to create every project in this book. Learn these and you will be a sewing diva in no time!

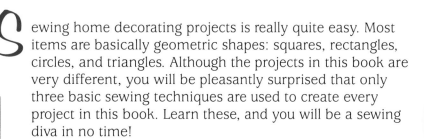

Sewing home decorating projects is really quite easy. Most items are basically geometric shapes: squares, rectangles, circles, and triangles. Although the projects in this book are very different, you will be pleasantly surprised that only three basic sewing techniques are used to create every project in this book. Learn these, and you will be a sewing diva in no time!

Your Sewing Fear Factor: Get Over It!

Does the idea of sewing leave you in tortured despair? Is your desire to learn how to sew blocked by your lack of confidence? Do the demons of decorating have control of your creativity? It's time to take charge and throw away those chains that bind. Just be fearless. Remember, you are the mistress of your sewing domain.

Take solace in knowing you are not the only one who has these fears. With this book, I am sitting right beside you and guiding you along the way. Trust your instincts, trust me, trust yourself, and you will have great results. Don't take yourself too seriously—consider sewing as a new playground where you are simply the new kid on the block. But you'll make friends quickly and have a beautiful home to show for it... Go for it!

Technique 1: Sewing A Seam

Yeah, I am making a big deal about stitching a seam. But seams are what hold your project together; they are the nuts and bolts of sewing. Stitch a good seam, and you will have a great end result!

Starting Out on the Right Foot

Whether you inherited your sewing machine or just bought a new one, chances are it came with an assortment of presser feet. Each foot is designed for a specific sewing task. The all-purpose presser foot is used for the majority of projects in this book (fig. 1). If the machine came with only one presser foot, it's probably this one. However, for the curtain projects, you may want to use a blind stitch foot for the hems (if available for your machine).

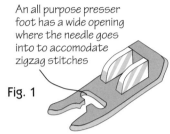

An all purpose presser foot has a wide opening where the needle goes into to accomodate zigzag stitches

Fig. 1

Paper to Project

Let's break down operating a sewing machine to the simplest — and most nonthreatening level. Begin by unthreading the machine and removing the bobbin. Then grab a piece of lined notebook paper. Use the paper as if it were fabric by stitching on the lines (fig. 2).

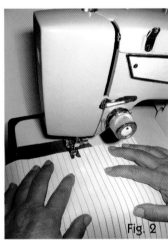

Fig. 2

This is a great way to get the feel of the machine as it stitches. Practice starting and stopping, stitching a straight line, and finding your own rhythm for raising and lowering the presser foot.

Gearing Up

Let's get your sewing machine set up to stitch a seam. Set your sewing machine as follows:

- Stitch: Straight

- Stitch length: 2 to 2.5 mm or 10 to 12 stitches per inch

- Stitch width: 0

- Needle position: Center

- Presser foot: All-purpose

- Seam width: $1/2$ inch (Identify the $1/2$-inch seam guide on the throat plate.)

Seam Team

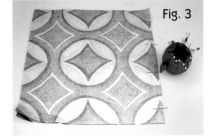

Fig. 3

1. Arrange two squares of fabric so they are right sides together with the edges even. Place straight pins in the fabric about every 3 inches and at a 90 degree angle to the cut edge of the fabric (fig. 3).

2. Raise the presser foot and the needle to its highest point. Arrange both the needle and bobbin threads to go under the presser foot (fig. 4) several inches. If the needle is not in its highest position as you begin to sew, the thread will probably come out of the needle.

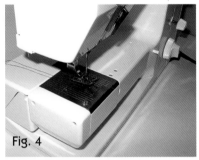

Fig. 4

3. Place the fabric under the presser foot and align the pinned, cut edge to the $1/2$ inch seam guideline on the throat plate. The bulk of the fabric is to the left of the needle. Manually

Fig. 5

turn the handwheel toward you and lower the needle into the fabric where the first stitch is to begin — $1/2$ inch from the top edge (fig. 5). The lowered needle will hold the fabric in place while you double-check the seam width and lower the presser foot. Starting $1/2$ inch from the edge allows you to backstitch to secure the seam.

4. Lower the presser foot. Then push the reverse button and backstitch a few stitches to the edge of the fabric by gently pressing on the foot

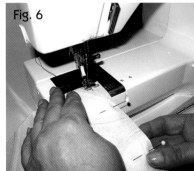

Fig. 6

pedal (fig. 6). *Don't forget to lower the presser foot.* If you forget, your fabric won't feed properly and you could really jam up your machine. This could lead to excessive cussing.

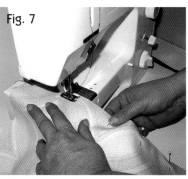

Fig. 7

5. Place your left hand lightly on top of the fabric so you can control it as you sew. Place your right hand 3 or 4 inches in front of the needle so that your fingers can guide the fabric edge. (Don't let your fingers get too close to the needle.) Let go of the reverse button. Then stitch forward at a slow, even speed, removing pins as you come to them (fig. 7). Do not pull the fabric while the machine is stitching; the fabric automatically moves forward because of the feed dogs.

6. At the end of the seam, press the reverse button and backstitch $^1/_2$ inch directly over the stitching. Stop stitching with the needle in its highest position (move the handwheel toward you if necessary) and then raise the presser foot.

7. Gently pull the fabric away from the needle at least 4 inches. Use the built-in thread cutter or relax the fabric slightly so there is a "dip" in the

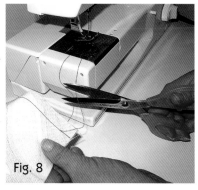

thread. Clip the thread (fig. 8). If you have to tug at the threads as you are pulling the fabric out from under the needle, raise the needle a little more until you can pull the fabric easily.

Fig. 8

Technique 2: Go to the Corner

Several steps are required to turn a corner precisely and create a sharply defined point or corner. To get the hang of it, practice on two pieces of fabric cut into 8-inch squares.

1. With your fabric marker, place a dot directly on the seam allowance $^1/_2$ inch in from the edge of the fabric (fig. 9). Place another dot $^1/_2$

inch away from this dot on the seam allowance (fig. 10). This second dot functions as a warning that you are near a corner.

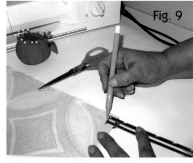

Fig. 9

2. Slow down when you come to the warning dot. Until you get the hang of it, remove your foot from the foot pedal and turn the handwheel toward you to

Warning Dot

Corner Dot

Fig. 10

stitch to the next dot. Stop with the needle down in the fabric exactly on the corner dot (fig. 11), raise the presser foot, rotate the fabric one-quarter turn, lower the presser foot and continue stitching (fig 12).

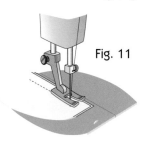

Fig. 11

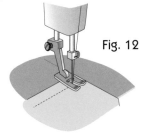

Fig. 12

PART 2 STITCH IT!

3. For reinforcement, stitch the corner section again directly over the previous stitching.

4. To eliminate bulk when the project is turned right side out, clip the seam allowance at the corner diagonally. Next, taper the seam allowances away from the corner: the sharper the point, the farther away from the corner the trimming should extend (fig. 13).

Fig. 13

Fig. 14

5. Turn the fabric right side out. At each corner, use a point turner to gently push the fabric out from the inside to create a sharp point (fig. 14).

The Bottom Line

Double hems are used when making window treatments. The extra weight of a double hem along the bottom edge makes the curtain or valance hang evenly. Double hems at the sides make a neat finish on both sides of the project. The cutting dimensions of your project must include a hem allowance that is two times the depth of the finished hem. This addition is reflected in the fabric calculations for the individual projects in this book.

Bottom Hem

Here's how to create a double 4-inch hem at the bottom of a curtain panel (fig. 15).

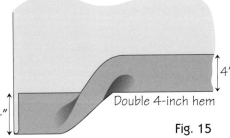

Double 4-inch hem

4"

4"

Fig. 15

1. Fold over and press 8 inches toward the wrong side of the fabric. To create a double 3-inch hem at the bottom of a valance, fold over and press 6 inches toward the wrong side of the fabric.

2. Tuck in the top edge of the hem to meet the fold and press.

3. Stitch along the folded edge with a straight or a blind hem stitch.

Side Hem

The side hem is created the same as the bottom hem, only it is a double 1^1/$_2$-inch hem. Here's how to create the hem at the sides of a curtain or valance panel.

1. Fold over and press 3 inches toward the wrong side of the fabric.

2. Tuck in the top of the hem 1^1/$_2$ inches to meet the fold and press.

3. Stitch along the folded edge with either a straight stitch or a blind hem stitch.

Technique 3: Blind Hem Stitch

A blind hem stitch is used to stitch hems in curtains. The stitch is a combination of several straight stitches and a zigzag stitch and is usually a built-in specialty stitch on your sewing machine. This stitch is used because it will not show on the front of the project you are making. Some machines recommend that you use a special blind hem presser foot. You can also use a presser foot that accommodates a zigzag stitch.

If your machine doesn't have a built-in blind hem stitch, you can use a straight stitch. However, if you are anal about things like not having stitches show on the front, you may want to stitch the hems by hand. (I can hear those moans now!)

Practice the hem stitch on a scrap fabric to get the hang of it. Here goes — let's stitch a double 4-inch hem.

1. Fold, press, and pin the double hem in place.

2. Place the hemmed edge of the project, hem side down, on the sewing machine bed. Fold back the body of the sample project to expose the top inside edge of the hem (fig. 16).

3. Begin the stitch on the hem edge. Do not backstitch at the beginning and end of a blind stitch hem. The straight-stitch portion of the stitch goes on the hem

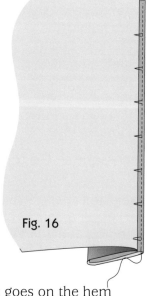

Fig. 16

STITCH IT!

edge and the zigzag stitch swings over and "bites" into the folded back portion of the fabric. The width of the zigzag stitch determines the amount of thread that will show on the front of the project. (The stitches on the front should be as inconspicuous as possible.)

4. After the project is hemmed, press the hem flat.

Technique 4: Pressing Matters

Okay. I know I said you needed to know only three sewing techniques to sew all the projects in this book. Well, technically, pressing is not a sewing technique, but I couldn't send you off without mentioning the importance of pressing as you sew. In my mind, everything goes together.

Most fabrics pucker slightly when stitched. If a seam is really puckered, the finished project will look messy or it won't lie or hang straight. That's why it's important to press each seam as it is stitched — to smooth the fabric and return it to its prestitched state as much as possible.

Ready, Set, Press

Usually, the instructions will say, "press the seam open" or "press the seam to one side" before continuing with the project. This is how you press the seam open:

1. Arrange the project, wrong side up on an ironing surface.

2. Set your iron to the appropriate temperature according to the fabric content.

3. With your index and middle fingers, open the seams so the seam allowances lay flat. Using

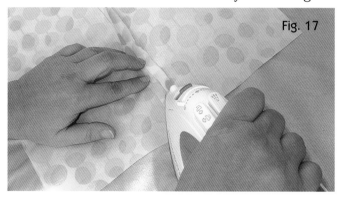

Fig. 17

HOME DEC BECK SAYS:

- Always start with an empty bobbin. Never wind one color of thread over another color.

- Don't wind the bobbin so full that it is hard to insert into the bobbin case. Many machines have an automatic shutoff feature when the bobbin gets full. If yours does not, be careful not to overfill the bobbin. (The thread should not be flush with the edge of the bobbin.)

- The thread on the bobbin has to be evenly wound across the bobbin spool for the machine to operate properly.

- For the projects in this book, always use the same thread for both the top and bobbin thread.

- Every time you change the bobbin, use a tiny brush to remove any lint that may have built up inside the bobbin case.

PART 2
STITCH IT!

the tip of the iron, press the seams so the seam allowances stay open without the help of your fingers (fig. 17).

4. Lift the iron and move to another section until the entire seam is pressed open.

5. Make sure the seams are flat. The seam should be neat on both sides of the fabric.

6. From the front side, examine the seam closely. You should almost see the stitching between the two folded edges of the seams.

Technique 5: Cinch of a Stitch

All right. I am slipping another technique in here. I can count, but again I think this is an important enough step to highlight. I suggest a little handsewing on many of the projects in this book. This handstitch, called a "slip-stitch," is what I recommend for closing seams on pillows, place mats, table runners, and other projects.

1. Thread an 18-inch length of thread through a handsewing needle. Pull through about 8 inches.

Stitching Successfully

Here are some sewing tips for a successful project.

- For all projects in this book, use a $1/2$-inch seam allowance unless otherwise instructed.

- Stitch a few test seams to determine the correct stitch length for your fabric. If the seam puckers, try adjusting the stitch length. A seam that puckers even slightly will prevent a window treatment from hanging straight.

- Always place pins perpendicular to the edge of the fabric with the pin heads toward the cut edge. Do not sew over the pins. However, if you feel you absolutely need to stitch over a pin, turn the handwheel toward you until you are past the pin.

- Use extra-long straight pins with large heads so they are easy to see. Forgotten pins can become enclosed inside hems or other areas that have been stitched closed.

- Backstitch at the beginning and end of each seam to secure stitches. To backstitch, take a few stitches in reverse, then continue forward for the remainder of the seam.

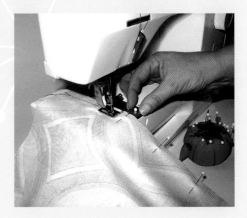

- Trim all loose threads as you stitch a seam.

- Do not consider the selvage (the tightly woven finished edge) as part of the seam allowance. A seam that includes the selvage may pucker. Therefore, cut off all selvages before constructing any project.

Tie a knot at the other end by wrapping the thread around your index finger. Then, using your thumb, roll the thread off your finger. The thread will twist itself into a knot.

2. Slide the needle under the seam allowance; bring it to the outside of the seamline. If you are right-handed, stitch from right to left; if left-handed, do the opposite. Pull the thread gently until the knot catches under the seam.

3. Insert the needle into the folded edge of the seam allowance just ahead of where you brought the thread out. Run it under the fold for $1/2$- to $3/8$-inch, then bring the needle out and pull until the thread is taut. Take your next stitch in the opposite fold; insert the needle directly across from the previous stitch (fig. 18).

4. Continue in this rhythm until the opening is closed. Stitch a little past the opening. Take several *tiny* stitches on top of each other in the

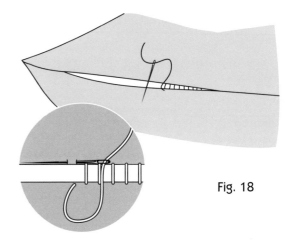

Fig. 18

seamline to knot the thread. Then take one long stitch under the seam allowance, bring out the needle in the seamline and cut the thread close to the surface. The thread tail will disappear inside the project.

9 | Behind the Seams

This chapter is titled perfectly — it explains the specifics of what goes on behind the seams before you start to sew your project. After reading these tips, you will zip through the projects!

I know you are dying to jump right into your project. You are probably thinking, "Heck with this chapter — I just wanna sew!" Remember my **More Splash Than Cash®** decorating philosophy I explained in the introduction? That to save time and money it's better to work smarter? So, stay with me here.

A lot of what is in this book is probably new to you (or you need a refresher course because it's been a very long time since you sewed). This chapter is titled perfectly — it explains the specifics of what goes on behind the seams before you start to sew. After reading these tips, you will zip through the projects!

Prep School

The rule of thumb for preparing fabrics for sewing is to clean the fabric exactly the way you will clean the finished project. For example, if you plan to wash the project in a washing machine, then wash the fabric before making a single cut into it. If you plan to dry-clean the project (as many fabric manufacturer's recommend), then you need to send the fabric to the dry cleaner beforehand. Why go through this process?

Fabrics made with natural fibers shrink when dry-cleaned or washed (even if cold water is used). And if the fabric comes into contact with heat (either steam or the dryer), the fabric will shrink even more. By preparing the fabric *before* making a project, you will avoid later disappointments. This process is called "preshrinking."

However, I don't always preshrink fabric. I take it project by project. For example, if I am making curtains using 54-inch home decorating fabric... I just dive into my project. I figure that I've paid for the special finishes applied to my fabric and I don't want my money to go down the drain (literally and figuratively). Besides, I don't wash my curtains.

Now, the story is different if I am using 100 percent cotton craft or quilting fabric and am making a pillowcase for my nephew or napkins for a dinner party. Since this type of fabric doesn't have special finishes, I preshrink the fabric. Besides, I know the pillowcase and the napkins will be washed often.

Now, back to the curtains. I don't wash the curtains (or anything made from decorator fabrics, for that matter). But I do clean them regularly. I vacuum them to remove any dust and surface dirt. Or I toss the item into the dryer on a low temp along with a sheet of fabric softener or a damp wash cloth. It comes out clean and refreshed.

So the decision whether to preshrink the fabric is yours.

Knowing Right from Wrong

The right side of the fabric is the side you want to see or the prettier side. On printed fabrics, it's usually very easy to tell the right side from the wrong; the wrong side is usually very muted in color and not very attractive. However, it is sometimes difficult to tell the right side from the wrong when the design is woven into the fabric. In that case, choose the side you like best but make sure you use the same side as the right side throughout the project. To avoid confusion, place a piece of masking tape on the right or wrong side of the fabric.

Whatever you decide, cut the fabric with the right side up so you can see the designs easily and plan your project accordingly. Keep

Both sides of this fabric are interesting—use the side you like best or consider it to be reversible.

in mind that sewing how-to illustrations (including the ones in this book) show the right side of the fabric in a darker shade than the wrong side.

Press Pass

These pressing tips are important to understand before, during, and after making your project.

- *Ironing* is a sweeping motion and is only used to remove wrinkles from the fabric.

- *Pressing* is an up and down motion where the iron is applied to the surface and then lifted completely off of the fabric and moved to another position. Seams are pressed open.

- Give your iron a thorough cleaning before starting your project. Special iron-cleaning creams are available in the notions department of your fabric store. Follow the manufacturer's instructions to clean your iron.

- Remove any pins before pressing your project so they won't scratch the iron.

- Always use the appropriate temperature setting for the fabric you are pressing. Cottons require a hot temperature setting, and synthetics require  a cool setting. Blends are somewhere in between. If the fabric content is unknown, test a range of settings on scraps of fabric, with and without steam. Check for press marks or shrinkage. If the finish is damaged or if water spots are visible, adjust the temperature.

- When changing iron temperatures, be sure to allow enough time for the iron to reach the desired temperature.

- A press cloth can prevent ironing disasters such as the fabric becoming scorched or shiny. Place a press cloth on the decorator fabric so the iron does not come in direct contact with the fabric. Use a scrap of fabric to determine whether you get better results with a dry iron and a moist press cloth or a steam iron and a dry press cloth.

A Cut Above

Regardless of whether you are cutting out a square for a pillow or a length of fabric for a curtain, these hints will assure that you will cut a clean, straight, and crisp line.

- Hold sewing shears with two fingers through the long, oblong hole and thumb through the smaller, round hole.

- If you are right-handed, cut with the majority of the fabric to the left of your scissors (reverse if you are left-handed). This way you will be able to see any cutting lines.

- The fabric should be smooth with no ripples or folds. It should lie flat on the cutting surface (not draped over the edge). Cut one layer at a time. More than one layer can slip, and the result will be pieces of different sizes.

- Allow the fabric to remain relaxed and flat when cutting it. Pulling may distort the fabric and prevent accurate cutting.

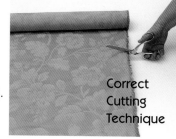

Correct Cutting Technique

- For the straightest line, always keep the bottom blade of the shears against the cutting surface at all times. Do not lift the fabric to cut. Raising it off the table when cutting can leave you with a zigzag edge.

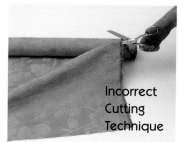

Incorrect Cutting Technique

- Use your shears to their maximum advantage and cut using the full length of the blades. Cut with long, steady strokes. Do not take small, short strokes or the edge will appear "choppy."

Cut It Out!

Does just thinking of cutting into your beautiful fabric cause your palms to sweat and heart to beat so fast you think it is going to pop out of your chest? Relax, take some deep breaths, and follow these guidelines. Then you'll breeze through this step when it comes to making your project.

- Before cutting into your fabric, determine its printed direction by studying the design. The direction of a design with flowers, stems, and leaves is easy to discern, but other fabric designs may not be so obvious. Many fabrics have a directional arrow printed on the selvage to help you determine the direction of the print.

- Work on a flat surface. This can be a table for smaller projects. You may have to clear floor space for larger projects. I have been known to cut fabric outside on the patio!

- From a straightened end of the fabric, measure the cut-length measurement (determined in your project) along the selvage and place a mark. Then measure it again. That's right! Do everything you can to catch any mistakes now before the fabric is cut.

- After each fabric length is cut, snip a small corner off the top of each panel so you can quickly distinguish between the top and bottom.

Rotary Cutting

Rotary cutting is a time-saving technique when cutting several layers of fabric. To have a complete rotary cutting system, you need an acrylic 6-inch-by-24-inch ruler, a special self-healing cutting mat, and rotary cutter. If you want to experiment with these cutting tools, get into the habit of closing the cutter after each and every cut. The blade is unbelievably sharp, and rotary cutter accidents can happen quickly. Respect this tool as you would any other sharp object, such as kitchen knives, saws, or razor blades.

For Good Measure

You are probably going to ignore my advice and cut your fabric without double-checking your measurements. It seems that every sewer has to learn the importance of measuring the hard way. It's like this is a rite of passage into some sort of sewing sisterhood. But I'm going to tell you this again anyway:

The axiom "measure twice, cut once" is aptly applied to every sewing project. You will have to cut the fabric too short only once to truly know how important this statement is.

PART 2
STITCH IT!

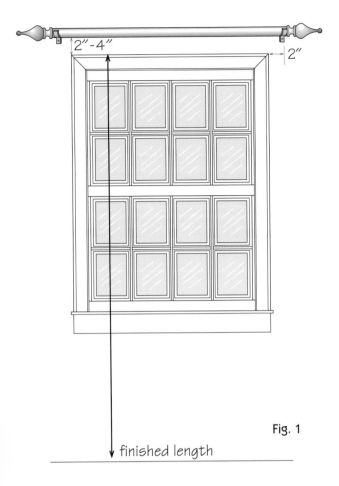

Fig. 1

finished length

Window Treatments

- When measuring for window treatments, mount the hardware before taking any measurements.

- The hardware should be mounted 2 to 4 inches from the top and side edges, of the window (fig, 1) and not on the window frame itself (if at all possible). The wooden frame could split and that is not easily fixed.

- Floors can be uneven and windows out of plumb (crooked), so measure for the finished length of floor-length curtains at several places across the width of the window. Use the shortest measurement as the finished length so the curtain doesn't buckle at the bottom edge.

- To measure for a floor-length curtain and the floor is carpeted, lay a piece of cardboard over the carpet to get more accurate measurements.

- For accurate measurements, use a stepladder to reach the top of the window. Use a retractable metal tape measure, not a cloth or plastic one (which stretches). Have someone else hold one

end of the tape measure in position when you're taking measurements.

- Write down all measurements as you determine them so you can keep these figures always close at hand. Check every measurement twice before cutting into the fabric.

Duvets and Comforters

Comforters vary in size from manufacturer to manufacturer — there is no such thing as a "standard size." If you compare two queen-size comforters from two different manufacturers (or even the same manufacturer), the dimensions may be completely different. Don't rely on the measurements that are printed on the tag or on the bag the comforter comes in — they are many times wrong.

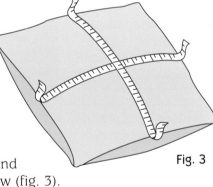

width

length

Fig. 2

To get the most accurate measurements, lay the comforter flat on the floor. Measure its length and width from outside edge to outside edge (fig. 2). Use a metal tape measure for accuracy.

Pillows

Don't rely on the measurements printed on the bag the pillow form comes in — they are many times wrong. Measure both the length and width of the pillow (fig. 3).

Fig. 3

Use these measurements to determine the cutting dimensions for your pillow cover.

Get Ripped!

Mistakes are bound to happen — even the most talented sewers find themselves ripping out stitches. Ripping out stitches is never fun, but it's a part of sewing. Somehow it is comforting to know that no seam is permanent! A seam ripper is really helpful to remove unwanted stitches. However, you will have to be very careful so that you don't accidentally cut your fabric in the process. (In case you do — all is not lost, just refer to chapter 11 "HELP!").

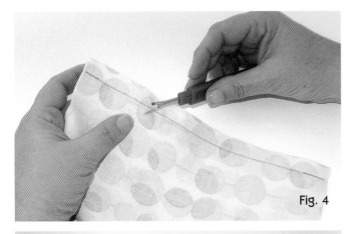

Fig. 4

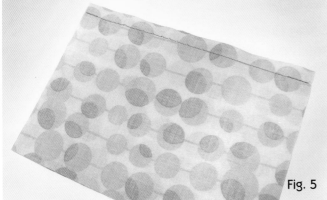

Fig. 5

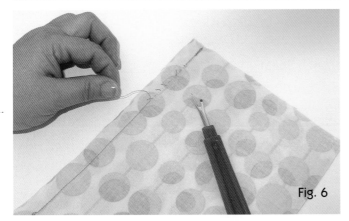

Fig. 6

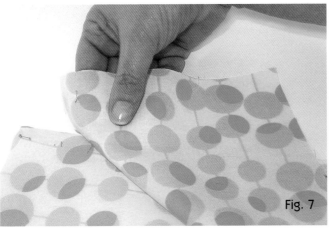

Fig. 7

1. Working from the top side of the seam (which means the seam allowance is to the right of the stitching), insert the longest point of the seam ripper under the middle of a stitch; make sure you don't catch the fabric. Gently push the seam ripper forward until the thread is cut (fig. 4). The blade is the horseshoe shape of the tool.

2. Continue to cut every 2 or 3 stitches the length of the area you want removed (fig. 5).

3. Turn the fabric over and pull the thread—it should come away from the fabric with very little effort (fig. 6). Separate the two pieces of fabric (fig. 7). Brush off any loose threads.

All the Fixins'

After you've ripped out the stitches, how do you fix the seam? If you had to rip out the entire seam, you simply restitch it. However, if you only had to rip out a section, here's how you proceed:

1. Make sure all loose threads are removed from both sides of the seam.

2. If the seam was pressed open, press it closed (that means to press the seam allowances together) (fig. 8).

3. Begin to stitch by lowering the needle four or five stitches above the removed stitches *directly on the remaining stitch line.*

4. Stitch as if you are stitching a seam; stop directly on the existing stitches four to 5 stitches $^1/_2$ inch below the removed stitches (fig. 9).

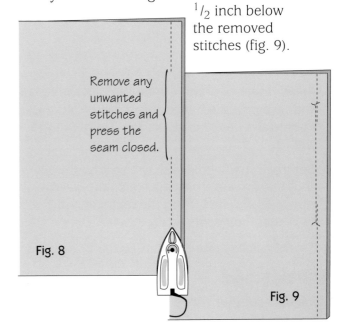

Remove any unwanted stitches and press the seam closed.

Fig. 8

Fig. 9

Take Cover

Covered buttons are a perfect finishing touch for some of the projects in this book. Commercial kits are available to make round or square covered buttons. Decorative frames are also available to further enhance the covered button.

How to Make a Round or Square Cover Button

1. Cut a square or circle from the fabric using the pattern on the package.

2. Place the fabric, right side down, into the button mold (this comes with the button forms).

3. Arrange the fabric around the form with your fingers (fig. 10).

4. Snap on the back.

Fig. 10

5. A decorative frame can be added by snapping it over the fabric-covered form.

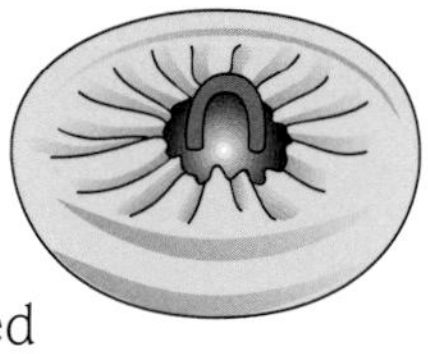

Sewing on Buttons

This is the easiest and fastest way to sew on a button! Use a sharp needle with an extra-large eye.

1. For each button, cut a piece of carpet or waxed thread 18 inches long.

2. Tie the thread to the shank of the button (fig. 11). Both thread ends should be even in length.

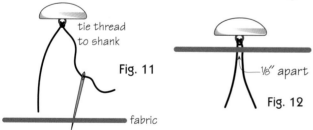

tie thread
to shank

Fig. 11

⅛" apart

Fig. 12

fabric

3. Insert one end of the thread through the needle and take one stitch with this thread from the front to the back of the project. Unthread the needle.

4. Rethread the needle with the second thread end. Stitch from front to back so the needle comes out $^1/_8$-inch from the first stitch (fig. 12). Unthread the needle again.

5. Tie the threads into a knot. Clip the thread ends.

Finishing School

If you are working with a fabric that frays easily, you may need to apply a seam finish — especially if you plan to wash your project. Here are the three methods that I like the best:

Pinking Your Edges

Use pinking shears and cut along the raw edge of the fabric seams (fig. 13). The pinking shears will cut little zigzags into the fabric. These diagonal edges prevent the seams from raveling. This method works best on woven fabrics.

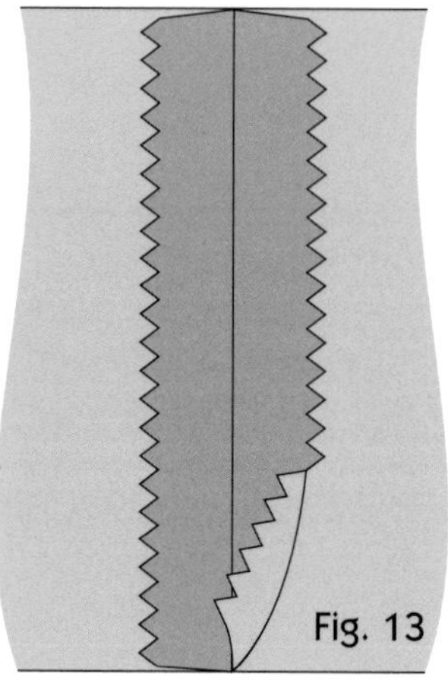

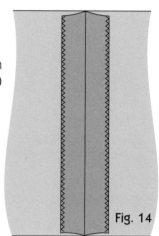

Fig. 13

ZigZag Finish

Stitch the edge of the fabric before stitching the seams. Set your machine to a wide zigzag stitch with a stitch length to 2.5 (or 10 stitches per inch). Stitch close to the cut edge of the fabric so that the right side of the zigzag stitch goes over the edge (fig. 14). If the fabric puckers, change the stitch width.

Fig. 14

French Seam

A French seam is used when there is no fabric (or lining) to cover the wrong side of the fabric. The edges are enclosed in a sealed seam. Here's how to sew a French seam:

1. Place the fabrics wrong sides together. Stitch a seam using a $^1/_4$-inch seam allowance.

2. Trim the seam allowance to $^1/_8$ inch, and press the seam to one side.

3. Fold the fabric so the right sides are together and the seam line is enclosed in the folded edge. Stitch another $^1/_4$-inch seam, encasing the $^1/_8$-inch edge in the seam (fig. 15).

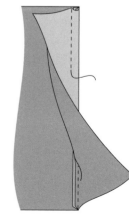

Fig. 15

PART 2
STITCH IT!

10 | Home Dec Tech

This chapter explains some special construction details that are exclusive to home decorating projects.

S ome specific procedures are unique to home dec sewing. We've already learned the three basic sewing techniques. This chapter explains specific details that will result in a well-constructed project (like how to join fabric widths together to get the size you need or how high to hang a curtain rod over the window). Don't worry about keeping all of these details stored in your noggin; the techniques that are used in each project, along with the page numbers where they are explained, are listed with the project.

Let's Get This Straight

In theory, fabric needs to be "on grain." The grain of the fabric refers to the direction of the threads. Being on grain means that the crosswise threads are perpendicular to the lengthwise threads.

Ideally, the printed pattern should align with the grain line. In reality, few fabrics are printed precisely on grain. In fact, it is more common to find the design to be printed off grain as much as $1\frac{1}{2}$ to 2 inches. Fabric mills consider this amount to fall within their acceptable range of print deviation. If stripes and plaids are printed off grain, the error is especially obvious.

Pulling the fabric (described in step 5 on the next page) may partially or completely correct the situation. However, many decorator fabrics have finishes applied to the surface. Consequently, the threads are more secure and cannot be easily manipulated.

**PART 2
STITCH IT!**

53

Follow these instructions to straighten the design on your 54-inch-wide decorating fabric.

1. Work on a large, flat surface. Place the fabric right side up.

2. Bring the selvages together, and fold the fabric so that it lies flat without ripples and the motifs match. Make a small snip with scissors in the selvages through both layers. If the motifs don't match, go to step 5 now for further instructions.

3. Open the fabric to a single thickness, right side up. At the snip, align one blade of a carpenter's square along the selvage (fig. 1). Using the other blade as a straightedge, draw a line across the width of the fabric.

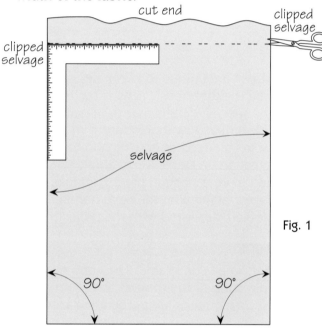

Fig. 1

4. Ideally, the line will connect to the snip at the opposite edge, forming a perfect right angle with the selvage. You can consider the fabric ready to use.

5. If the selvages don't match or if the line is slightly off the snip at the opposite selvage 1 inch or less (fig. 2), you may be able to straighten the design by pulling the fabric. Trim

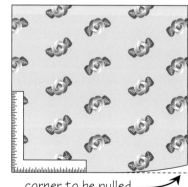

corner to be pulled ➞

Fig. 2

the selvage from the side that appears short. Then pull the fabric from that corner to the opposite diagonal corner (fig. 3). For fabric longer than 2 yards, work by pulling shorter diagonal sections. If all attempts to straighten the design are unsuccessful, and the difference is still more than $1/2$ inch, consider using another fabric.

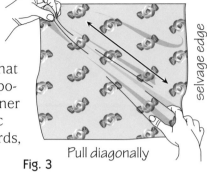

Pull diagonally

Fig. 3

Worth Repeating

Examine the selvage of 54-inch decorator fabric to identify a repeat (a "repeat" is the distance from one motif to another that is exactly the same). Find a distin-

Fig. 4

guishing feature of the printed motif and scan along the selvage until you see the same feature (fig. 4). The distance can vary from 1 to 36 inches or more. Many times a plus sign, printed on the selvage will identify the start and stop of a repeat.

If your fabric has a prominent repeat design, determine where the design will be placed on the finished project. For example, if you are making multiple pillows or shams, the same motif should be in the same position on each pillow front. For more information on placing designs on your projects, refer to "Fussy Cutting" on page 55.

Repeat after Me

To cut additional widths, use the first length as a guide. Place it directly on top of the remaining fabric, right sides up, matching motifs (fig. 5). Use a straightedge and fabric marker to mark the cutting line.

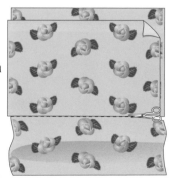

Fig. 5

To cut matching pillow or sham fronts, cut the first one to size. Then place it directly on top of another area of the fabric and match the designs on all four cut edges to the uncut fabric (fig. 6). Pin the cut piece in place and cut around it.

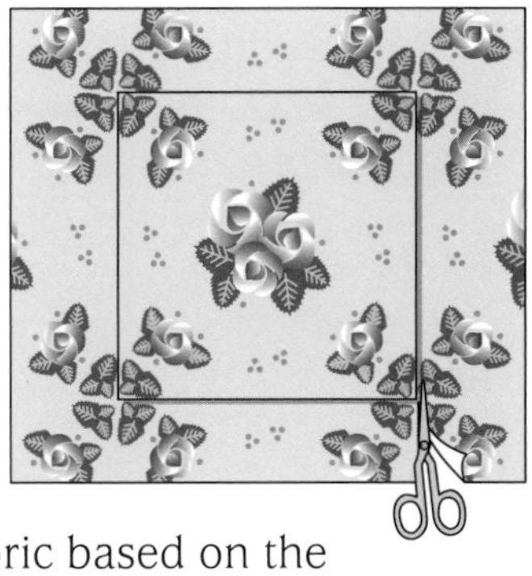

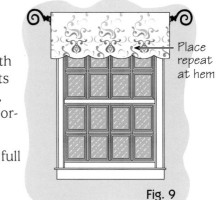

Fig. 6

Fussy Cutting

Fussy cutting is when you selectively cut the fabric based on the fabric's pattern design repeat rather than cutting randomly into the fabric. For example, if you want to place a certain section of the design at a speci- fied position on the project (like centering a flower in the middle of a pillow top) and you cut the fabric to accomplish this, this is called "fussy cutting."

Fussy cutting is the preferred method of cutting when making home decorating items because of the placement of the repeats. When planning your project, determine where a full repeat design should be placed for maximum effect. This is using the fabric design to its highest potential.

Window Treatments

Consider placing the fabric design at the following positions for this all-important home decorating component.

- For floor-length curtains, place one full design just below the top finished edge; this is where the eye travels first (fig. 7). Don't forget to allow fabric above the design for any finishing (such as hems) the project calls for.

- For sill and apron length curtains and shades, the place-

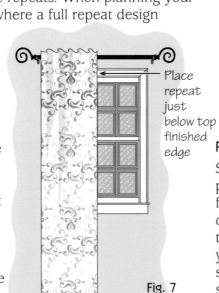

Place repeat just below top finished edge

Fig. 7

Place repeat at hemline

Fig. 8

ment is just the reverse — one full design should be even with the finished bottom hem edge (fig. 8). Don't forget to allow extra fabric below the design for the hem allowance.

- If you have both floor- and sill-length window treatments in the same room, then follow the floor- length guideline.

- For a valance, the full design should be along the bottom finished edge (fig. 9).

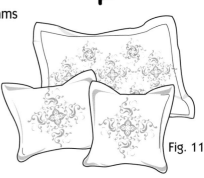

Place repeat at hem

Fig. 9

Duvet Covers

- The top edge of the design should fall any- where between $1/3$ to $1/2$ below the top edge of the mattress (out of the way of the pillow shams) (fig. 10).

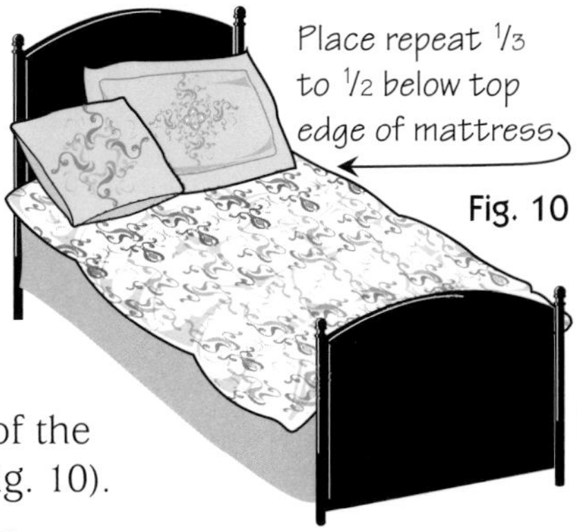

Place repeat $1/3$ to $1/2$ below top edge of mattress

Fig. 10

Pillows and Pillow Shams

Select the most prominent, or your favorite, part of the design and place that in the center of your pillow or pillow sham. All pillows should be made the same (fig. 11).

Fig. 11

The Great Divide

For large home dec sewing projects, such as curtains, a duvet cover, or a shower curtain, more than one fabric width is needed to obtain the size. Sometimes, both full and half-widths are used. A half-width is what it sounds like (it's a full width of fabric cut in half lengthwise). Here is the easiest way to cut a half-width of fabric.

1. Fold a cut length of fabric in half lengthwise with right sides together and selvages even.

2. With an iron, press a hard crease on the fold.

3. Open the fabric. With the fabric flat on the work surface, cut exactly on the pressed crease (fig. 12).

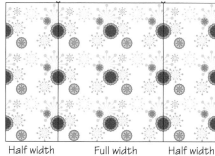

Fig. 12

Split Personality

When joining multiple widths or half-widths of fabric, you need to determine the seam place-ment. This depends on what type of project you are making. Don't worry if the combined widths are wider than you need—they will be cut to the correct measurement after the widths of fabric are joined (see "Cutting It Down to Size," page 57).

Duvet Cover

• Usually 2 widths of fabric are needed to make a duvet cover. Place the full width in the center and stitch a half-width to each side of the full width (fig. 13).

Full Length Curtains

The number of fabric widths needed for a window treatment is based on the width of the window and how full you want the curtains to be. To create the fullness, you simply sew one or more widths together. Here's how.

• If $1\frac{1}{2}$ widths are required to make a curtain panel, the half-width is stitched to the outside edge of each full width (fig. 14).

• If 2 full widths are required to make a curtain panel, stitch the widths together side by side (fig. 15)

• If 3 full widths are required to make a curtain panel, stitch the widths together side by side (fig. 16).

Fig. 13 –
Two widths of fabric ▶

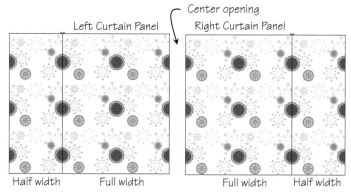

Half width   Full width   Half width

Fig. 14 –
$1\frac{1}{2}$ widths per curtain panel ▼

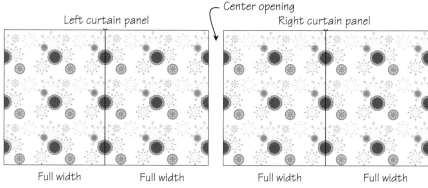

Left Curtain Panel   Center opening   Right Curtain Panel

Half width   Full width   Full width   Half width

Fig. 15 –
Two widths of fabric per curtain panel ▼

Fig. 16 –
Three widths of fabric per curtain panel ▶

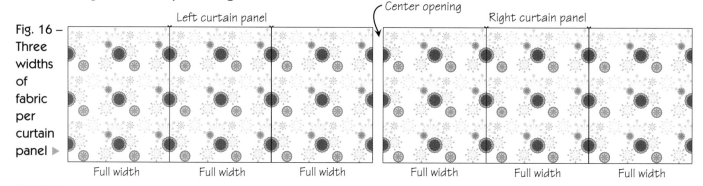

Left curtain panel   Center opening   Right curtain panel

Full width   Full width   Full width   Full width   Full width   Full width

Valance

- If 2 full widths are required to make a valance, one full width is in the center and a half-width is stitched to each side of the full width (fig. 17).

- If 3 full widths are required to make a valance, stitch the widths together side by side (fig. 18).

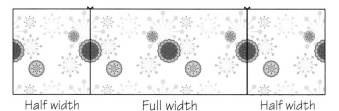

Half width Full width Half width

Fig. 17 – Two widths of fabric ▲

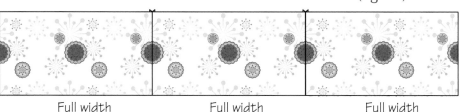

Full width Full width Full width

Fig. 18 – Three widths of fabric ▲

Matchmaking

Extra fabric is needed to match the designs at the seams (determined in the fabric calculations) for each project. I like to use a technique called "fuse basting" to match the fabric designs. This is done with paper-backed fusible tape. This product is found in the notions area of the fabric store. Check the information printed on the packaging. *It's essential to use a tape that can be stitched through;* some adhesives can gum up the needle. Follow these instructions to fuse baste a seam.

1. Lay the full width of the fabric on a large work surface right side up. Remove the selvages (fig. 19).

Fig. 19

2. Press the cut edge of one fabric toward the wrong side. Place a strip of paper-backed fusible tape, adhesive side down, on this pressed edge, close to the fold (fig. 20). Follow the

Fig. 20

package instructions for iron temperature and steam setting. Iron the paper side of the tape; allow it to cool and then remove the paper.

3. Arrange the fabric panels so they are both right side up. Working from the top to the bottom, lap the pressed seam allowance over the unpressed one; match the motifs exactly (fig. 21). Then fuse the fabrics together (fig. 22).

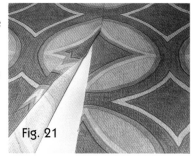

Fig. 21

Fig. 22

4. Now arrange the panels so they are right sides together. Stitch directly on the pressed line (fig. 23) and the motifs will be perfectly matched! Press the seam to one side.

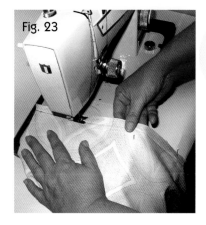

Fig. 23

Cutting It Down to Size

To trim the joined fabric widths to the cut-width measurement, trim equal amounts of fabric from both side edges (fig. 24). If you cut the excess from one edge only, the design and seams will be lopsided.

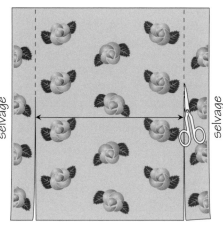

selvage

selvage

Fig. 24

PART 2 STITCH IT!

Lining Up

Lined window treatments have many advantages. While you may incur some additional cost, lining extends the life of the window treatment, enhances its appearance, increases insulation, and makes lightweight fabrics hang better.

Lining provides more privacy and reduces the amount of light, noise, and dust that filter through a window. Lining also hides construction details. I determine how to line a window treatment by its location. If it is for a front-of-the-house window, which means the window faces the street or other public area, I always line the window treatment with white or off-white lining. This gives the windows a unified appearance from the street (called "curb appeal"). However, if the window is a back-of-the-house window, I am much freer with the color of the lining (if I line at all).

Support System

Think of hardware as the bone structure of your window treatment. The correct hardware will aid in the proper fit and the visual appearance of the finished treatment.

- Buy good-quality hardware from a reputable manufacturer. Don't try to save money by buying bargain brands; they usually aren't sturdy enough.

- Enlist a partner to help you install drapery hardware. Two sets of eyes are better than one when deciding on placement and two sets of hands make the installation easier.

- Match the visual weight of your hardware to that of the window treatment you are making. Generally, the heavier the fabric, the larger the rods should be; thinner rods work well with silks or sheers.

- If you'll be placing hardware over an existing window treatment, such as a shade, allow for clearance between the layers (at least 2 inches).

- The curtain rod must be level for the curtain to hang straight. The only way to determine if the rod is truly straight is to use a level.

- The most secure place to mount your hardware is into a stud. Usually wooden 2-by-4s surround each window opening. The easiest way to find

these studs is to knock firmly on the wall with the heel of your clenched fist. A solid sound means that you have located a stud; a hollow sound tells you to keep knocking. Once you've found the studs around the window, mark them at the level you plan to hang the brackets.

- If you can't mount your hardware into a stud, use wall anchors for additional support for the rod. Window treatments can be awfully heavy, and you do not want the rod to come out of the wall after the curtains are hung!

The Right Height

Hung up on the right way to hang your curtains? Ideally, mount the hardware at each window before taking any measurements for your window treatment. You'll get more accurate measurements. Keep these points in mind when planning the window treatments in this book.

- The top edge of a clip-on curtain or valance should be even with the top edge of the window frame. Slide the rings with the clips onto the rod to determine where to hang the rod before taking any measurements.

- All floor-length curtains should finish $1/2$ inch above the floor so they don't drag. Don't stop them midway between the window and the floor or they will appear skimpy, not stylish.

- The rod for the large grommet–style curtain is placed 2 to 4 inches above the window frame.

- "Café" curtains are half-length curtains and are hung from a rod mounted at the middle of the window. The bottom edge of this casual style "kisses" the windowsill.

- Valances are a shorter version of curtains that adorn the top of a window. The finished length varies but should be about $1/5$ to $1/6$ the distance from the rod to the floor.

- Camouflage the shape and size of your window by extending the rod several inches outside of the window frame. This will make your window appear wider. You can also mount the rods at the ceiling to make your window appear taller.

"There are no such things as screwups in sewing—only design opportunities."

11 | *Help!*

I sincerely hope you never have to use this chapter! But it's here just in case you do.

Consider this: It's the middle of the night. You are so into your project that you've lost all track of time. Then suddenly, your machine turns into a monster or you cut something wrong. What's a girl to do? It is comforting to know that you are not alone in this "sewing hell." Here are some common problems and easy solutions to get you over your initial panic. "HELP!" stands for "Help for Every Little Problem." I sincerely hope you never have to use this chapter! But it's here just in case you do.

Fixing Common Sewing Goof-Ups

There is nothing worse than spending hours on a project only to goof it up in the end. But believe me, all sewers have been there. That's where experience comes in! I've compiled a list of "things that can go wrong" and offer my solutions. I believe that everything can be fixed. The result might not be what you wanted to begin with, but usually something wonderful can be salvaged.

OOPS!

Cut the corner off!

TO THE RESCUE!

Stitch a second seam slightly inside the first line of stitching

Problem: Corner Cut Wrong

You cut the fabric corner too severely when trimming a corner.

Solution

Make the project smaller. For example, stitch another seam around the edges an even distance from the edge. Yes, the project may be somewhat smaller, but not by that much.

Problem: You Poked A Hole With Your Point Turner

When you're pushing out a corner from the inside, the point turner accidentally pokes through the fabric and creates a small hole.

Solution

Turn the project right side out and examine the hole. It could be that the yarns of the fabric were just separated by the point turner and there's no actual hole. If that is the case, use your fingernail to lightly scratch the threads to rearrange them and close the hole. For added reinforcement, apply a little dab of liquid seam sealant directly over the spot (on the wrong side of the fabric).

If a definite hole was created, see the solution for trimming a corner too severely.

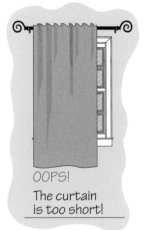

OOPS!
The curtain
is too short!

Problem: Curtain is Too Short

After the curtain is installed at the window, you discover it is too short.

Solution

There are several possible solutions to this situation, depending on the severity of the miscalculation.

- Try the window treatment on another window in the same room. Sometimes the windows look like they are exactly the same, but they are not. You might get lucky.

- Redesign the window treatment to include a wide band of coordinating fabric along the bottom edge. Remove the hem and stitch a new band to the bottom edge. This will turn your mistake into quite a design statement!

TO THE RESCUE!
Open the hem and add a band of coordinating fabric to the bottom edge

- If possible, lower the curtain rod until the curtain falls at the length you want and add a valance to cover the top edge.

- Ideally, a hem is 4 inches deep. Instead of tossing the entire project into the trash and thinking you are a complete failure, just make the bottom hem narrower.

- As a last option, place a chair or another piece of furniture in front of the window treatment to disguise the hemline.

Problem: Cut Fabric by Accident

You accidentally cut a slit into the fabric, either with a seam ripper or with scissors.

Solution

Use a piece of fusible interfacing (as small as possible, but still large enough to cover the slit on all sides). Make sure the slit is closed and the design matches, and fuse the interfacing to the wrong side of the fabric. Then act like it isn't there and continue with your project.

Trouble Shooting Machine Problems

The first thing to remember whenever things are not going your way is: most sewing machine problems are caused by two things — *there's a problem with the needle or the machine is threaded incorrectly.* So before you take any drastic steps, insert a brand new needle and/or completely rethread the machine (including the bobbin).

The Machine Stitches in One Place and the Fabric Doesn't Feed

Here's what to check.

- Did the stitch length get switched to 0?

- Is the presser foot completely lowered?

- Are the feed dogs up and able to catch your fabric?

Scorch mark from the iron!

Problem: Scorched Fabric While Ironing

You got distracted while pressing your project and left the iron on the fabric too long. Consequently, you now have an iron-shaped image on your project.

TO THE RESCUE!
Make a matching "patch" from fabric and paper-backed fusible web

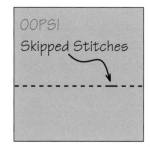
TO THE RESCUE!
Fuse the new patch over scorch mark

Solution

Okay, I'll admit this is trickier to fix. The simplest solution is to cut a patch from left over fabric that is just large enough to cover the scorch mark and carefully fuse it directly on top of the area. Cut the patch so the fabric design matches the design on your project exactly. Don't confess your mistake, and no one will know the difference!

- If both the presser foot and feed dog are in the correct position, the presser foot may have too much or too little pressure. Refer to your manual to adjust.

The Needle Will Not Move

Here's what to check.

- Did you remember to disengage the bobbin winding mechanism?

- Is the presser foot up?

The Needle Breaks

What causes this? Here's what to check.

- The needle may break if it stitches over a pin.

- Check to see if the needle is inserted straight. Is it all the way up into the needle bar? Is the needle clamp screw tight?

- Is the needle too small or not the correct type for the fabric you are using? For example, are you using a needle specifically for a sheer fabric to sew on leather?

- The presser foot may not have been placed on your machine correctly and it is loose.

- Check your sewing technique. Do you pull the fabric as you sew? Let the fabric flow naturally under the presser foot. The slightest bend in the needle can cause the needle to snap.

Skipped Stitches

A skipped stitch looks like one or more stitches are extra long as compared to the others. Why does this happen?

- The machine and/or the bobbin case may not be threaded properly.

- The needle could be bent, blunt, the wrong size, or inserted wrong. Change the needle immediately. Discard the old needle.

OOPS!
Skipped Stitches

- Make sure the thread you are using is a quality name brand because poor quality thread can cause skipped stitches.

- The thread tension may be too tight. Adjust it slightly (see Tension Trouble Shooting, page 62).

- If the problem continues, and you have checked all of the above, take the machine to a dealer for service. The timing may be off.

Puckered Seams

What causes this problem?

- The stitch length may be too long for your fabric. Make an adjustment and then stitch a test seam.

- The needle may be blunt. Change it immediately even if the needle is brand new. Needles are pretty inexpensive!

OOPS!
Puckered Seam

- The top tension may be too tight. Check with your manual to loosen the tension slightly.

PART 2 STITCH IT!

Upper Thread Breaks

What should I do?

- Rethread the sewing machine completely (including the bobbin).

- The needle could be bent, blunt, the wrong size, or inserted wrong. Remove and replace the needle immediately.

- The thread tension may be too tight. Loosen the upper tension slightly (see Tension Trouble Shooting).

Bobbin Thread Breaks

What causes this?

- The most probable cause is that the bobbin is wound incorrectly. If it is, remove all thread and then rewind it so it is smooth and wound at an even tension.

- Take out the bobbin from the bobbin case completely and then reinsert it.

- When was the last time you cleaned the bobbin compartment? The bobbin case may be dirty with lint.

Holes Appear in The Fabric at Each Stitch

What causes this?

- If holes are visible in the fabric where the stitches are, the needle is probably too large for the fabric.

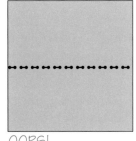

OOPS!
Holes appear at each stitch

Tension Trouble Shooting

If you have determined the tension needs adjusting (after changing the needle and rethreading the machine), always adjust the top tension first. The tension on a sewing machine is simply a matter of balance and small adjustments can make a big difference. Don't be intimidated to adjust either the top or bobbin tension. Be patient — it is a matter of trial and error.

Fixing the Top Tension

If the top tension is too tight, the top thread is straight and the bobbin thread has formed loops on the top side of the fabric. To correct, begin by loosening the top tension (moving the tension dial counter clockwise). You may have to adjust the top tension knob a half turn or more before you'll see any impact on the thread tension. If you have loosened the top tension and not seen an improvement, then the bobbin tension may also need to be adjusted.

Fixing the Bobbin Tension

If the bobbin tension is too tight, the stitches will appear with bobbin thread straight and the top thread looped on the underside of the fabric. The bobbin case tension is much more sensitive than the top tension and should only be adjusted about 1/8 of a turn at a time. Use a small screwdriver to adjust the screw on the side of the bobbin case. In addition, you may need to tighten the top tension.

To check your bobbin tension, place a fully wound bobbin into the bobbin case. Hold the bobbin thread between two fingers and let the bobbin case dangle. If the tension is correct, the bobbin case will stay in place. If the bobbin case slides down the thread, the tension is too loose.

Simple Tension Test

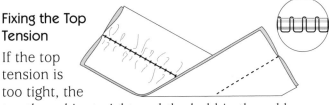

Thread the machine with one color thread in the top and another color in the bobbin. Cut a 5-inch square from the fabric you are using to make your project. Fold it in half diagonally to form a triangle. Finger press the fold to form a crease. The diagonal line is the bias of the fabric. It stretches slightly. Stitch a line along the bias fold.

Grasp the stitching between your thumb and index finger (your hands should be about 3 inches apart) and pull quickly with even force until one of the threads breaks. If the broken thread is the color of the thread in the needle, it means that the top tension is too tight. If the broken thread is the color of the bobbin thread, the top tension is too loose. If both threads break together and take more force to break, it means that the tensions are balanced.

PART 2
STITCH IT!

PART 3: Make It!

You can't buy individual style, but you can make it!

My goal with this next section was to provide you with super easy yet stylish projects that will work in any room in your home. The lines are clean and simple and will really show off the fabric you choose. I selected these projects and wrote the directions to ensure your success.

I am providing you with methods, not just a recipe for a project. And after learning the sewing process for each project, you can make simple measurement changes and create other projects. Suggestions for additional projects that can be made with only minor changes are listed under the section named "Multiple Choices" with each project. Just imagine all the possibilites.

Now you can change your mind, change your mood, and change your décor on a whim—all because you've learned to sew!

TABLE OF CONTENTS:

A tower of mock box pillows is an intriguing and versatile accessory.

HOME DEC BECK SAYS:

"Never underestimate the power of pillows. They can punch up any space with color, comfort, and attitude."

1 | Soft Landings

STITCH UP FOUR DECORATIVE PILLOWS

Even budget-conscious decorators can indulge their fabric fixation by making a profusion of pillows. Pillows are to home dec sewing what scarves are to knitting: the perfect project to start with. Pillows add instant impact to any room in a home and can push your creative juices to the max while keeping costs to a minimum. Once you get the hang of constructing a pillow, there are no limits to what you can create.

Multiple Choices

Don't think pillows are just for the bed or sofa! After reading this chapter, you will be able to make any kind of pillow you can think of. A basic square pillow can be as tiny as a potpourri sachet for your dresser drawer or as large as a floor pillow to plop on in front of the TV. Change the shape to a rectangle and you can make any thing from the daintiest boudoir pillow to a snuggly body pillow. By incorporating the simple boxing technique you'll learn later in this section, you can transform a square pillow into a rectangle and make a bench cushion for your home or deck, a mattress for a futon, or a cushion for your favorite outdoor lounge chair—even a new bed for your favorite furry friend!

Before You Begin

We're starting with the basic square pillow (*A Square Deal*). Next, you'll discover how easy it is to change the pillow front from a solid square into an easy geometric pattern (*The Right Angle*). This pillow uses two different fabrics. Finally, you'll learn how to make a mock-box pillow that adds a stylish element to your pillow collection (*Boxing

Match and *Stay Tuned*). The *Stay Tuned* pillow features a special pocket to stash your iPod® as you snooze.

Round Up

Now, let's get started and gather the following:
– Home dec sewing kit
– Decorator fabrics (see individual projects)
– Thread to match decorator fabric
– Fleece-type batting
– Muslin
– Pillow form
Optional: loose fiberfill

Fabric Swap

Suggested fabrics for these projects include drapery-weight cotton fabric, quilt-weight cotton fabric, silk, corduroy, velvet, and chenille.

Go Figure

Need help measuring? Here's where to find it. How to Measure a Pillow, page 50

On the Cutting Edge

Before cutting into your beautiful fabric, review these cutting tips.
– Fussy Cutting, page 55
– Cut It Out, page 49

PART 3
MAKE IT!

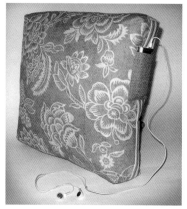

The Right Angle (left)
A Square Deal (right)

Stay Tuned

A Square Deal, Boxing Match, and Stay Tuned

1. *For all pillows:* Measure your pillow form. Add 1 inch to both the length and width measurement for the cutting size. For example, if your pillow measures 16 inches square, your cutting size is 17 inches square. If you are using a rectangle pillow of any size, use the same formula.

2. From the decorator fabric, cut one front and one back. You do not have to use the same fabric for both the front and back. Mix it up if you want to make it reversible!

3. Cut two shapes the same size as the pillow fabric from the fleece-type batting and muslin.

4. *For Stay Tuned:* In addition to step 2, cut a rectangle 5 inches by 7 inches for the pocket.

The Right Angle

Use two coordinating fabrics and cut the following:

- For a 14-inch finished pillow, cut two squares, each 17 inches.

- For a 16-inch finished pillow, cut two squares, each 19 inches.

- For a 18-inch finished pillow, cut two squares, each 21 inches.

- For a 20-inch finished pillow, cut two squares, each 23 inches.

- For a 24-inch finished pillow, cut two squares, each 27 inches.

- For a 30-inch finished pillow, cut two squares, each 33 inches.

1. Regardless of the size pillow you are making, cut both squares into quarters diagonally (fig. 1).

2. Cut two squares 1-inch larger than the finished size of the pillow from the fleece-type batting and muslin.

Fig. 1

Gearing Up

If you need help setting up your sewing machine, refer to page 42.

It's Sew Time!

The directions for each pillow are so similar, I didn't want to keep repeating myself. So when you see the name of the pillow you are making in a step, do that step. Then go to the next step that includes your pillow's name.

Need to brush up on your sewing skills? Here's where to find help.
- Seam Team, page 42
- Pressing Matters, page 45
- Go to the Corner, page 43

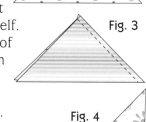

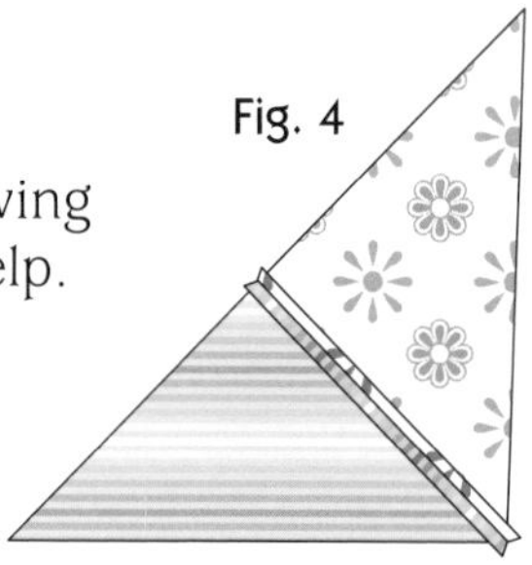

Fig. 2

Fig. 3

Fig. 4

Fig. 5

1. *The Right Angle.* Arrange the triangles as shown in fig. 2. Stitch the two sets of triangles together (fig. 3). Press the seams open (fig. 4). Then place the combined triangles right sides together and stitch the long edge (fig. 5). Press the seam open. Repeat for the back.

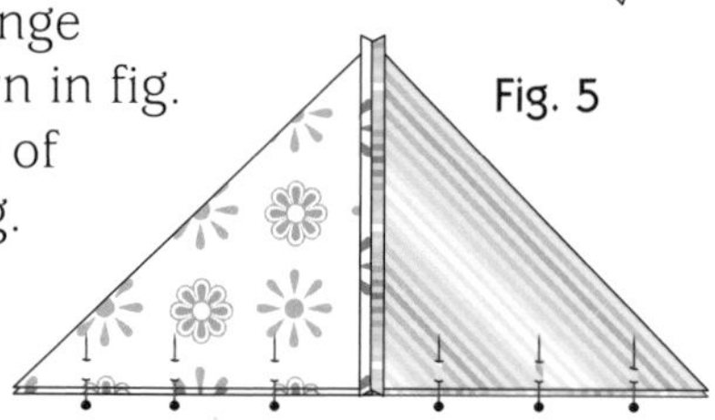

2. *For all pillows:* Place the fleece-type batting and muslin on the wrong side of both the pillow front and back (fig. 6).

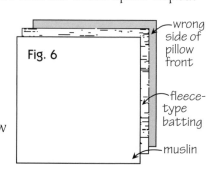

Fig. 6

wrong side of pillow front

fleece-type batting

muslin

3. *Stay Tuned* (steps 3, 4, and 5): Place the front and back right sides together matching all raw edges. Stitch along one side of the pillow only. Press this seam open.

4. Prepare the pocket by folding the rectangle in half with right sides together so it measures $3\frac{1}{2}$ by 5 inches. Stitch 1 inch from the top along the cut edge; backstitch. Then stitch 2 inches from the bottom along the cut edge; backstitch (fig. 7). Press the seam open. Arrange the pocket so the seam is in the middle and facing up (fig. 8).

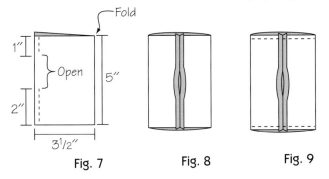

Fig. 7 **Fig. 8** **Fig. 9**

Then stitch across the bottom and top edges (fig. 9). Through the seam opening, turn the pocket right side out and press it flat.

5. Center the pocket where desired over the seam on the right side of pillow. Stitch around three sides of the pocket, leaving the top edge open (fig. 10).

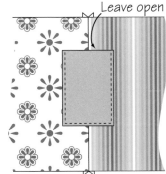

Leave open

Fig. 10

6. *For all pillows*: Pin the front to the back, right sides together, matching all raw edges. Mark 8-inch opening on one side.

7. *For all pillows*: Lower the needle at the $\frac{1}{2}$-inch seam allowance

Fig. 11   8″ opening

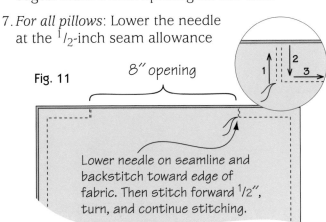

Lower needle on seamline and backstitch toward edge of fabric. Then stitch forward $\frac{1}{2}$″, turn, and continue stitching.

More Splash Than Cash® Decorating Tips

Pillows are an inexpensive and colorful way to add colors, shapes, and textures to your home. Pillows soften the lines of contemporary furniture and add splashes of color where needed. Pillows are a good way to change your decorating schemes on a whim—and on a budget.

• Pillow fronts can be created from decorator fabrics, a needlepoint project, or an interesting piece of tapestry fabric. Sometimes you can splurge on fabric for a pillow front and select a less expensive, coordinating fabric for the backing.

• Pillows are perfect decorating accessories for kids' room. They can also be tossed on the floor for portable seating for visiting friends.

• Play with texture. Whether it's soft felt, crisp linen, cool cotton, or luscious velvet, make your pillows from fabric that will tempt you to touch them.

• Play with the arrangement of your pillows. Line the pillows up symmetrically, stack them by size, or toss them randomly. Can't decide? Change it every week.

on one side of the opening. Maneuver the pillow cover so the $\frac{1}{2}$-inch seam allowance is parallel with the front edge of the sewing machine (fig. 11). Backstitch to the edge of the fabric, then stitch forward to where you first lowered the needle. Keep the needle down in the fabric and pivot the fabric to the regular sewing position. Continue stitching around the pillow until you get to the other side of the opening. Finish the stitching at this side of the opening as you did at the beginning.

8. *Square Deal* and *The Right Angle*: Trim excess fabric away from the corners.

PART 3 MAKE IT!

HOME DEC BECK SAYS:

Squaring Off

"To make a square pillow, (such as *A Square Deal* and *The Right Angle*) the pillow cover isn't exactly square. Stay with me, because this technique really works!

Cut the pillow front and back (including fleece-type batting and muslin) in a square to fit your pillow. Place fabrics right sides together. Before stitching, line up the straight edges of the pillow corner template (pictured) with the cut edges of the fabric. With a fabric marker, trace along the template's curved corner edges. Also mark the new corner pivot point provided on the template. Repeat this process at the remaining corners. Cut the fabric on these marked lines through all layers (the centers of each side remain unchanged). Stitch around the pillow following the newly cut edges (don't forget to leave an opening). Turn the pillow cover right side out. The cover will look odd, but once the pillow form is inserted, the pillow will appear square. Ta Dah!"

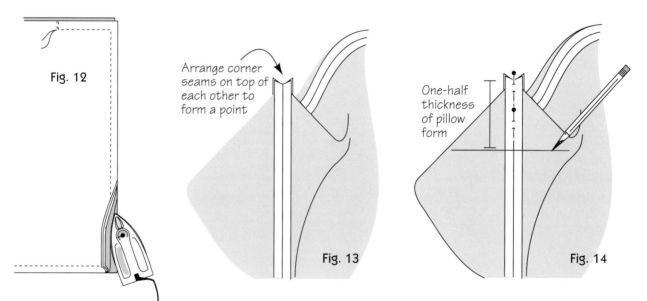

Fig. 12

Arrange corner seams on top of each other to form a point

Fig. 13

One-half thickness of pillow form

Fig. 14

9. *For all pillows*: Go to your ironing board and turn back the top seam allowance (against the muslin). With the tip of the iron, apply light pressure down the crease of all seams (fig. 12).

10. *Boxing Match* and *Stay Tuned*: Place one hand through the opening and to one corner. Separate the front fabric from the back and arrange the corner so the seams are on top of each other, forming a point (fig. 13). Pin the layers together to secure them. Measure from this point one half the thickness of the pillow form and mark this measurement directly on the seam. Draw a perpendicular line across the seam from fold to fold at this mark (fig. 14).

Stitch on the marked line; backstitch at the beginning and end of the seam (fig. 15). Trim the excess fabric to $1/2$ inch from the stitched line. Repeat at all corners.

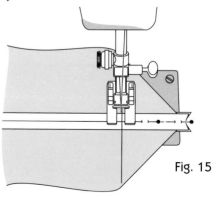

Fig. 15

11. *For all pillows*: Turn the pillow cover right side out through the opening. With the point turner, go in through the opening and push out the corners to make them as smooth as possible (fig. 16).

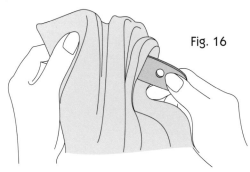

Fig. 16

12. *For all pillows*: Compress the pillow form and insert it into the opening. Arrange the pillow form so that it is smooth on all sides. If needed, fill the corners with loose fiberfill stuffing for a nice finish.

The Finish Line

To see how to add some finishing touches, refer to these sections for details.
– Cinch of a Stitch, page 45
– Take Cover, page 52

1. You will notice that the seams at the opening are already folded toward the inside. This is because of the technique we used when stitching around the pillow. Pin these edges together and slip stitch the opening closed.

2. *Optional*: Add a covered button in the center of the pillow (fig. 17). The covered button in the photo includes a decorative frame.

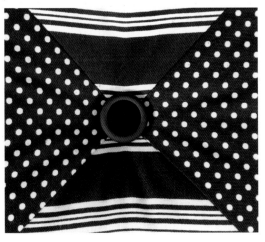

Fig. 17

HOME DEC BECK MINI-PROJECT:

" Make your own pillow forms with quilt batting and loose fiberfill stuffing. Now you will have no limitations on the size and shape of any pillow you design. Here's how."

Form Flattering

- From the batting cut two outer layers 1 inch larger than the pillow top.
- Cut four more pairs of layers, each 2 inches smaller than the previous pair.
- Separate and stack the layers by sizes into two piles with the largest layer on the bottom of each pile.
- Place the two piles together with the smallest layers together in the center. Baste around the edges of the pillow to hold the layers in place. Wrap this bundle with another piece of batting and stitch closed.
- After you insert the form into the pillow cover, fill out any empty pockets (such as the corners) with loose fiberfill.

▶ u dzine it

Since decorating is all about your individual style, here are some ideas for making your one-of-a-kind-pillows:

- Stitch together an assortment of neckties and make into a pillow front.
- Print favorite photos onto special inkjet fabric (available at craft and fabric stores) and incorporate them into your pillow.
- Look at your wardrobe for a piece of clothing that you still love but no longer wear. Cut out a section or two for your pillow.

Using the mock box technique, you can make a cushion for an outside bench.

PART 3
MAKE IT!

Layer your table runner over an extra-wide table shawl that substitutes for a tablecloth but with more style. A table shawl is the width of the table and any length you want.

HOME DEC BECK SAYS:

"Whether you are a foodie who loves to cook or a self-appointed queen of takeout, you should definitely have a beautiful place to dine!"

PROJECT 2 | Reservations Not Required

EASY TABLE RUNNER AND PLACE MATS

A table runner keeps a table fashionably dressed at all times—day or night. By having several styles in your decorating arsenal, you will always be prepared for unexpected guests or impromptu dinner parties.

Place mats are just smaller versions of table runners and are one of my favorite projects to sew. Now, I don't know about you, but I am pretty fuzzy in the morning before I have my java jolt. Sitting groggily at my kitchen table while my coffee brews is much more pleasant if I have a colorful place mat in front of me. Place mats are super quick and easy to make, and with all the unique fabrics available, I can make place mats to suit any of my moods or decorating desires. They're great for last minute gifts, also!

Multiple Choices

Table runners, a staple of easy and inexpensive decorating, are more versatile than you think! Of course, they make a dining or kitchen table look fabulous, but any surface they adorn will come instantly to life. Who woulda thought you could do so much with a lined strip of fabric?

- Top off a dresser, a hutch, a coffee table, an end table, a kitchen island, or an armoire with a runner made with gorgeous fabrics.

- Position one vertically over each sofa or chair cushion to add color and interest.

- A super narrow one will work as a mantel drape; an extra-wide one can become a slip-cover for a headboard.

A table shawl adorns this fireside dining table creating a warm and cozy decorating statement.

- Lay a runner across the bottom of your bed for a splash of color.

- If you make a table runner long enough, use it as a window topper—just add clips to the long edge and slide it onto a decorative rod.

- Reversible napkins and the beautiful chair covers on page 76 are sewn the same way as *Making a Run for It*.

Before You Begin

This section starts with instructions for a basic table runner *(Making a Run for It)*, where sewing is the simplest and the fabric is the star attraction. Next I will show you how to mix it up a bit and make the runner even more decorative by using four fabrics *(Dinner is Served)*. And, finally, I'll show you how to make an easy place mat *(Head of the Table)*.

PART 3 MAKE IT!

HOME DEC BECK SAYS:

"Have your friends over. Have your neighbors over. Heck, have your boss over, too. After a few hours of sewing, you will definitely have a beautiful table setting!"

Dinner is Served ▲

Making a Run for It ◄

Round Up

Now, let's get started and gather the following:
– Home dec sewing kit
– Decorator fabrics (see individual projects)
– Thread to match decorator fabrics
– Heavy- or craft-weight nonwoven fusible interfacing*
– Shells or beads (for *Making a Run for It*)
*Use for extra body if desired

Fabric Swap

For a casual table setting, drapery-weight cottons or quilt-weight cottons work best. For a dressy table setting, consider using velvet, velveteen, dupioni silk, a color-infused paisley, or embroidered silk. Heavier-weight fabric used for upholstering can be sewn into a beautiful runner. Check out the many theme fabrics available for special occasions and holidays.

Go Figure

Making a Run for It

Measure the length of your table (including the drop on both sides) to determine what size runner to make. The runner should drop over the table approximately 6 inches to 8 inches on both sides, but it can be any length you want. The width of the table runner is also up to you, but it usually is anywhere from 13 inches to 18 inches wide, or a third of the width of your table. Regardless of what size you make, add a 1-inch seam allowance to the length and width measurements for the cutting dimensions. Purchase enough fabric to equal the cutting length for your runner. You can use the same fabric for the lining or make the runner reversible by using another fabric.

If your fabric is lightweight or you want the table runner to have more body, purchase enough fusible interfacing to equal the cutting length of your runner.

Dinner is Served

This table runner is made from four coordinating fabrics. From the leftover fabric, you can make matching place mats. This is like getting the place mats for free! (This is one of those times when I especially love to sew.) You need the

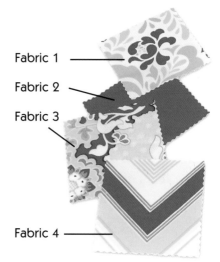

Fabric 1
Fabric 2
Fabric 3
Fabric 4

To help you determine your fabric choices, use these swatches as a guide.

PART 3
MAKE IT!

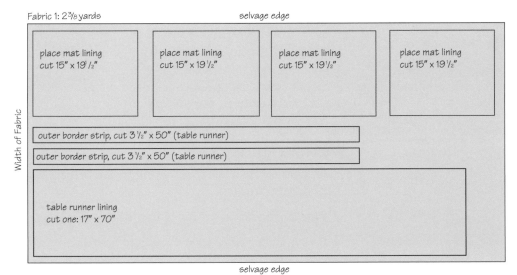

Fabric 1: 2³/₈ yards — selvage edge

Width of Fabric

- place mat lining cut 15" x 19¹/₂"
- place mat lining cut 15" x 19¹/₂"
- place mat lining cut 15" x 19¹/₂"
- place mat lining cut 15" x 19¹/₂"

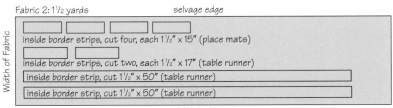

- outer border strip, cut 3¹/₂" x 50" (table runner)
- outer border strip, cut 3¹/₂" x 50" (table runner)
- table runner lining cut one: 17" x 70"

selvage edge

Fabric 2: 1¹/₂ yards — selvage edge

Width of Fabric

- inside border strips, cut four, each 1¹/₂" x 15" (place mats)
- inside border strips, cut two, each 1¹/₂" x 17" (table runner)
- inside border strip, cut 1¹/₂" x 50" (table runner)
- inside border strip, cut 1¹/₂" x 50" (table runner)

selvage edge

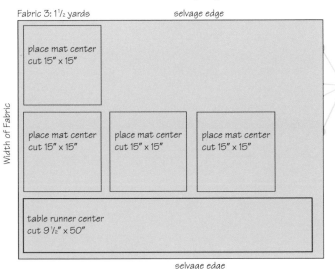

Fabric 3: 1¹/₂ yards — selvage edge

Width of Fabric

- place mat center cut 15" x 15"
- place mat center cut 15" x 15"
- place mat center cut 15" x 15"
- place mat center cut 15" x 15"
- table runner center cut 9¹/₂" x 50"

selvage edge

Fabric 4: ⁵/₈ yard — selvage edge

Width of Fabric

- table runner end cut 17" x 9¹/₂"
- table runner end cut 17" x 9¹/₂"
- placemat side band cut 3¹/₂" x 15"
- placemat side band cut 3¹/₂" x 15"
- placemat side band cut 3¹/₂" x 15"
- placemat side band cut 3¹/₂" x 15"

selvage edge

Fig. 1

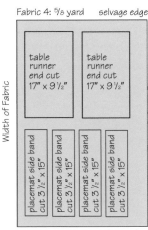

following (either 45- or 54-inch-wide fabric) to make a 16-inch by 69-inch runner and, with the leftovers, four *Head of the Table* place mats:

Fabric 1: 2³/₈ yards for outer border strip (also for lining)

Fabric 2: 1¹/₂ yards for inner border strip

Fabric 3: 1¹/₂ yards for center section

Fabric 4: ⁵/₈ yard for ends

Fusible interfacing: 2 yards

On the Cutting Edge

Before you cut into your beautiful fabric, review these cutting tips.
– Let's Get This Straight, page 53
– Cut It Out, page 49

Making a Run For It

1. Straighten one end of the fabric.

2. Using your measurements, cut two rectangles from the decorator fabric; the longest measurement is parallel to the selvage edge but don't include the selvage in measurement.

3. *Optional:* Cut one rectangle the same size as your fabric from the fusible interfacing.

Dinner is Served & Head of the Table

Refer to the layout (fig. 1) to make the most economical use of the fabrics so that you can make the table runner and four coordinating place mats.

1. From fabric 1, cut the following:

TABLE RUNNER
Two outer border strips, each 3¹/₂ inches by 50 inches
One lining strip, 17 inches by 70 inches

PLACE MATS
Four lining rectangles, each 15 inches by 19¹/₂ inches

PART 3 MAKE IT!

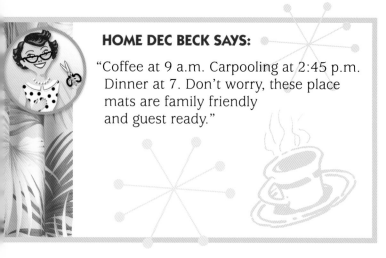

HOME DEC BECK SAYS:

"Coffee at 9 a.m. Carpooling at 2:45 p.m. Dinner at 7. Don't worry, these place mats are family friendly and guest ready."

2. From fabric 2, cut the following:

TABLE RUNNER
Two inside border strips, each $1^1/_2$ inches by 50 inches
Two inside border strips, each $1^1/_2$ inches by 17 inches

PLACE MATS
Four inside border strips, each $1^1/_2$ inches by 15 inches

3. From fabric 3, cut the following:

TABLE RUNNER
One center section, $9^1/_2$ inches by 50 inches

PLACE MATS
Four center sections, each 15 inches by 15 inches

4. From fabric 4, cut the following:

TABLE RUNNER
Two end pieces, each 17 inches by $9^1/_2$ inches

PLACE MATS
Four side bands, each $3^1/_2$ inches by 15 inches

5. For the table runner, cut one strip 16 inches by 69 inches from the fusible interfacing. For the place mats, also cut four rectangles, each 14 inches by $18^1/_2$ inches.

Gearing Up

If you need help setting up your sewing machine, refer to page 42, with the following exceptions:

Seam widths $1/_4$ inch and $1/_2$ inch (Identify the $1/_4$-inch and $1/_2$-inch seam guides on the throat plate.)

It's Sew Time!

Need to brush up on your sewing skills? Here's where to find help.
– Seam Team, page 42
– Go to the Corner, page 43
– Pressing Matters, page 45

Making a Run for It

1. Optional: Fuse the interfacing to the wrong side of one rectangle.

2. Pin the fabrics right sides together.

3. Proceed to "The Finish Line" (page 75).

Dinner is Served

Note: When sewing the fabrics together of this table runner, use a $1/_4$-inch seam allowance. Press all of the seams to one side.

1. Stitch the inside border strips to each long edge of the center section (fig. 2).

2. Stitch the two outer borders to the outside edges of the inside strips (fig. 3).

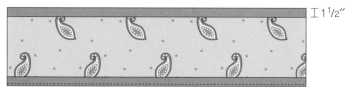

Fig. 2

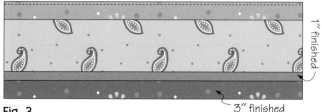

Fig. 3

3. Stitch the inside border strips to one long edge of both end pieces. Then stitch the pieces to each end of the center seam (fig. 4). Proceed to "The Finish Line" (page 75).

Fig. 4

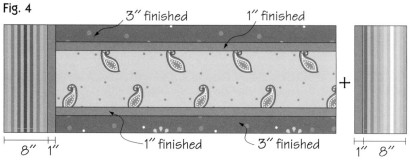

You don't need to wait for a special occassion to dress up your breakfast bar. I can't think of a better way to guarantee a good morning than having breakfast on bright and cheery place mats. These are so easy to make—you'll want to make them in many different fabric combinations.

Head of the Table

1. *Optional:* Fuse the interfacing to the wrong side of each place mat lining.

2. Using $^1/_4$-inch seam allowance, construct each place mat front as in fig. 5. Press the seams open.

3. Proceed to "The Finish Line."

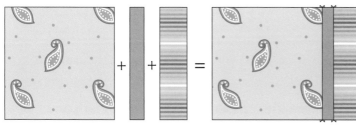

Fig. 5

The Finish Line

Need a quick refresher course on some finishing techniques? Here's where to find help.
– Go to the Corner, page 43
– Cinch of a Stitch, page 45
– Pressing Matters, page 45

1. Pin the front to the lining right sides together, matching all raw edges. Along one edge, deter mine where the opening will be. The opening should be at least 8 inches long.

2. Lower the needle at the $^1/_2$-inch seam allowance on one side of the opening. Maneuver the table runner or place mat so the seam allowance is parallel to the front edge of the sewing machine (fig. 6). Backstitch to the

PART 3
MAKE IT!

Fig. 6

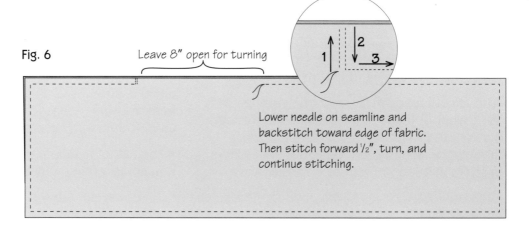

Leave 8" open for turning

Lower needle on seamline and backstitch toward edge of fabric. Then stitch forward $^1/_2$", turn, and continue stitching.

HOME DEC BECK MINI-PROJECT:

"This simple chair cover uses the same sewing techniques as a table runner. Depending on the fabric you select (use two different fabrics to make it reversible), this super easy project can take on many personalities. It's also a great More Splash Than Cash® way to bring color continuity to mismatched chairs."

1. Measure your chair seat. Measure the width of the seat along the back edge, the front edge, and the depth of the seat (from front to back). Also determine the "drop" measurement (how long you want the fabric to hang down from the chair seat).

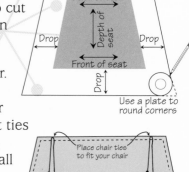

2. Draft your pattern with these measurements. First draw the seat shape then add the drop measurement to three sides. *Optional:* If you want rounded corners, use a salad plate as your pattern to create a smooth curve. Don't forget to add a $1/2$ inch seam allowance to all edges.

3. Before cutting into your fabric, you may want to cut the pattern from scraps to make sure the pattern you drafted fits your seat.

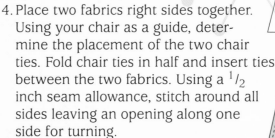

Use a plate to round corners

4. Place two fabrics right sides together. Using your chair as a guide, determine the placement of the two chair ties. Fold chair ties in half and insert ties between the two fabrics. Using a $1/2$ inch seam allowance, stitch around all sides leaving an opening along one side for turning.

5. Turn right side out, press smooth, hand stitch the opening closed and have a party!

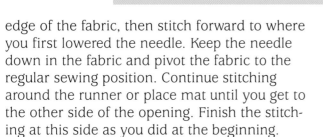

Place chair ties to fit your chair

Leave open for turning

edge of the fabric, then stitch forward to where you first lowered the needle. Keep the needle down in the fabric and pivot the fabric to the regular sewing position. Continue stitching around the runner or place mat until you get to the other side of the opening. Finish the stitching at this side as you did at the beginning.

3. Trim excess fabric away from the corners. Turn the runner or place mat right side out through the opening. With the point turner, reach through the opening and push out the corners to make them as smooth as possible.

4. Align the folded edges of the opening. Slip stitch the opening closed.

5. Press the runner or place mat smooth and flat. Make sure that neither fabric is visible from the opposite side along the stitched edge.

6. *Optional for Dinner is Served*: Handstitch shells or beads to the ends of the runner.

▶ u dzine it

Since decorating is all about your individual style, here are some ideas for making your one-of-a-kind table runners and place mats:

• Instead of a square end, design a new shape such as a point, zigzag, or round.

• Piece several fabrics randomly together for a place mat front.

More Splash Than Cash® Decorating Tips

Don't overlook the details when creating an exciting dining table for your family, friends, and guests to feast their eyes on!

- Layer several sizes of tablecloths or table runners in coordinating colors at different angles for an interesting base for dinnerware.

- The more the merrier applies not only to guests, but also to candles — especially when entertaining. Instead of lighting just one or two candles on the dining table, cluster a bunch of candles together for more impact. Or run them single file the length of the table.

- Use only one color to decorate your table. Flowers, plates, glasses, napkins, and table linens of the same color looks magnificent (and it's easy to do!)

- Arrange several table runners across the width of the table instead of down the length of the table. These table runners work overtime as place mats.

Fig. 7

Fig. 9

Fig. 8

Fig. 10

Make your runner or shawl reversible as we did here for even more versatility. Make sure the fabric weights are similar. Another trick is to stitch a fun trim to one side before sewing the front and back together. Then you have two completely different looks (Figs. 7 & 8).

Instead of a long, skinny rectangle, stitch up a square and place it diagonally on the table. Use two different fabrics for reversibility. Vintage-inspired rickrack adds extra personality and a dash of color (Figs. 9 & 10).

PART 3
MAKE IT!

Even though these curtains are simple to sew, they add wow to this bedroom. Made from vintage-inspired bark cloth, these curtains are really stylin'.

HOME DEC BECK SAYS:

"Create delicious eye candy for your window using a sassy print that tickles your fancy."

3 | Clippity-Doo-Dah

STYLISH CLIP-ON CURTAINS

Making your own window treatment is just one of the many ways to express your style as you decorate. This curtain is so simple in design and construction that the fabric becomes the star of the show. The great thing about this style of curtain: it looks great in any room of the home!

Multiple Choices

Don't think curtains as being just for the windows! You can use these same directions and make a curtain to use as a closet-door, a shower curtain, or a room divider. Using a tension rod, curtains can also substitute for cabinet doors in your bathroom or kitchen. Hang curtains on the wall behind your bed (with or without a headboard) to add instant height or additional color to your room. If you make this curtain style shorter, it becomes a café curtain or a valance.

Round Up

Now, let's get started and gather the following:
– Home dec sewing kit
– Decorator Fabric*
– Lining Fabric (optional)*
– Thread to match decorator and
  lining fabrics
– Decorative rod, mounting brackets,
  curtain clips, and finials
*Calculated to fit your window.

Fabric Swap

Suggested fabrics for this project include woven drapery-weight cotton fabric, cotton quilt-weight fabric, silk, jacquard, and lightweight chenille.

Go Figure

Need help measuring? Here's where to find it.
– How to Measure a Window, page 50
– Support System, page 58
– The Right Height, page 58

NOTE: Refer to the illustration (fig. 1) on page 80 for the fabric calculations.

1. Mount the rod above the window. Place the clips onto the rod. Measure from the top of the clip to the desired finished length. That's measurement A: ___.

2. For lined curtains, add $8^1/_2$ inches and that's measurement B: ___. For unlined curtains, add 12 inches. That's measurement BB: ___. Either B or BB is your cut-length measurement.

3. Measure the distance between the brackets and multiply this number by $1^1/_2$ or 2 (depending on how full you want the curtain to be). That's measurement C: ___.

4. The width of your fabric is measurement D: ___.

5. Divide (C) by (D). Round up to the nearest whole number to get measurement E: ___. This is the number of fabric widths you need to cut.

PART 3
MAKE IT!

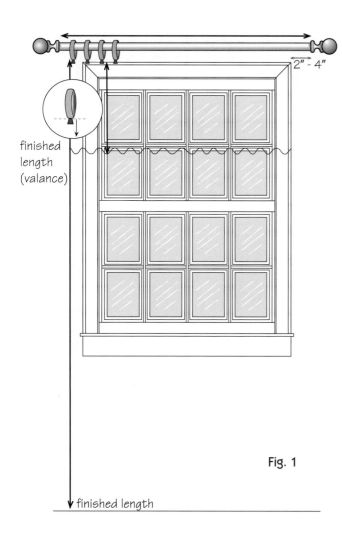

finished
length
(valance)

2" - 4"

Fig. 1

finished length

6. The fabric's repeat distance (if applicable) is measurement F: ___.

7. Add (B) or (BB) and (F) together. That's measurement G: ___.

HOME DEC BECK SAYS:

"I always use a French seam when making an unlined curtain. That way, no raw edges show on the wrong side of the curtain."

8. Then multiply (G) by (E) to get measurement H: ___.

9. Divide (H) by 36 inches for the total yardage needed for the decorator fabric.

On the Cutting Edge

Before cutting into your beautiful fabric, review these cutting tips.
– Let's Get This Straight, page 53
– Worth Repeating, page 54
– Fussy Cutting, page 55
– Repeat after Me, page 54
– Cut It Out, page 49
– The Great Divide, page 55

1. Straighten one end of the fabric. Cut one fabric width to the cut-length measurement (B) or (BB).

2. Using this width as a guide, cut additional fabric widths (E). Don't forget to match the design repeats as you cut the additional fabric widths.

3. *Optional*: Cut the same number of widths from the lining fabric.

Gearing Up

If you need help setting up your sewing machine, refer to page 42.

It's Sew Time!

Need to brush up on your sewing skills? Here's where to find help.
– Seam Team, page 42
– Pressing Matters, page 45
– Split Personality, page 56
– Matchmaking, page 57
– Lining Up, page 58
– Finishing School, page 52
– The Bottom Line, page 44

Unlined Curtain

1. Divide the decorator fabric widths to create two curtain panels according to the number of widths you cut. Then sew the widths right sides together to create separate panels; match repeats if necessary. Finish seams as desired (use a zigzag stitch, pink the raw edges, or make a French seam). Press the seams open unless using a French seam.

More Splash Than Cash

PART 3
MAKE IT!

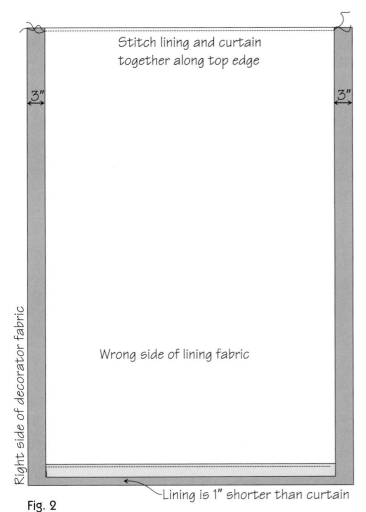

Stitch lining and curtain together along top edge

3"   3"

Right side of decorator fabric

Wrong side of lining fabric

Lining is 1" shorter than curtain

Fig. 2

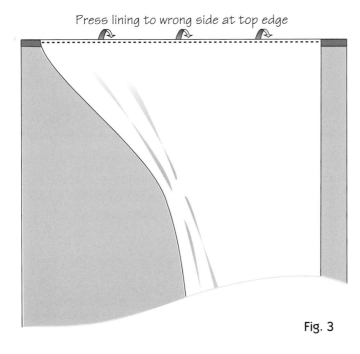

Press lining to wrong side at top edge

Fig. 3

HOME DEC BECK SAYS:

"Between pick-ups, drop-offs, and drop-ins, always find time to sew."

2. Hem the bottom edge of each curtain panel with a double 4-inch hem.

3. Hem the top edge of each curtain panel with a double 2-inch hem.

4. Hem all side edges with a double $1^1/_2$-inch hem.

Lined Curtain

1. Divide the decorator fabric widths to create two curtain panels according to the number of widths you cut. Then sew the widths right sides together to create separate panels; match repeats if necessary. Finish seams as desired (zigzag stitch or pink the raw edges). Press the seams open.

2. Stitch the lining fabric widths together. Then trim the lining fabric so it is 6 inches narrower and 3 inches shorter than each curtain panel.

3. Hem the bottom edge of each lining panel with a double 3-inch hem.

4. Hem the bottom edge of each curtain panel with a double 4-inch hem.

5. Center the lining over the curtain panel right sides together. The curtain panel should extend 3 inches beyond the left and right side edges of the lining. Pin, making sure the top edges of the decorator and lining fabrics are even and the bottom edge of the lining is 1 inch shorter than the curtain panel. Stitch the fabrics together along the top edge (fig. 2).

6. Bring the lining over to the wrong side of the curtain. Press the top edge smooth, including the remaining $1/_2$-inch top seam allowance that extends on each side of the lining (fig. 3). Stitch close to the top edge through all layers to prevent the lining from showing on the right side.

HOME DEC BECK MINI-PROJECT:

"I love to create things from surprising materials. So I headed to the plumbing department at my local home improvement store to see if I could find stuff to make a curtain rod. Here's what I came up with..."

Pipe Dreams

1. Attach an elbow to each pipe end. Then attach the extenders to the elbows. (Don't screw them too tightly in case you need to adjust them). The extenders are what make the curtain rod stick out from the wall.

Round Up

– Steel pipe ($^1/_2$-inch or $^3/_4$-inch diameter) the length you want the rod to be
– Two 90° steel elbows
– Two short steel extenders (for the part that protrudes from the window)
– Two steel floor flanges (2-inch or 3-inch diameter)
– Large head wood screws, $1\,^1/_2$-inches long

2. Place your curtain rings onto the rod.
3. Screw the floor flanges onto the open ends of the extenders.
4. Ask a helper to hold the entire unit in place while you screw the flanges to the wall.
5. Attach your curtain to the clips, hang and enjoy!

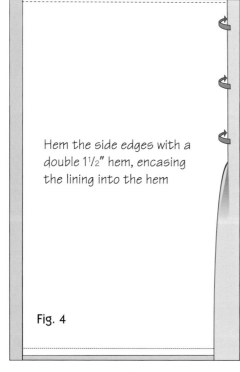

Hem the side edges with a double 1½" hem, encasing the lining into the hem

Fig. 4

7. Hem the side edges of each curtain panel with a double $1\,^1/_2$-inch hem, encasing the lining into the hem (fig. 4).

The Finish Line

Clip the rings to the curtains at even intervals. The farther apart the clips, the more the curtain will drape between the clips. Always use an even number of clips. Insert the rod through the rings. Attach the rod to the brackets. With your hands, arrange your curtains into attractive folds. This is called "dressing" your window treatment.

▶ **u dzine it**

Since decorating is all about your individual style, here are some ideas for making your one-of-a-kind clip-on curtain:

• Make a tricolor curtain by dividing the cut length into three sections. Don't forget to add a $^1/_2$-inch seam allowance to the edges of the sections.

• Decorate the finished edges of the curtain with ribbon or decorative trim.

• Instead of making one pair of curtains per window, make two pairs from different fabrics. Place one pair at the center of the window with the coordinating pair at the outside edges.

PART 3
MAKE IT!

More Splash Than Cash®
Decorating Tips

Hardware—once hidden—has become an important design feature in window treatments. However, traditional hardware can add significant cost to your project. So why not make your own? Here are some ideas to get you started.

- Bamboo poles are the perfect green solution to curtain hardware and are easy to hang curtains from.

- Create your own curtain rod from twigs, boat oars, fishing poles, tennis rackets, hockey sticks, rakes, ski poles, golf clubs, bamboo or copper torches, or fireplace tools. Hang the curtains from the newly fashioned hardware.

- Copper piping makes an interesting curtain rod. It is available at your local hardware store and can be cut to the exact length you need.

- Spray paint purchased rods in any color to match your décor.

- Transform wooden pole rods and finials into custom pieces by dyeing or staining them with fabric dye, or adding a decorative paint finish. Or cover the rod and finials with scraps of left over fabric, coordinated wallpaper, rope, twine, or decorative cording.

- Gather together doorknobs or smaller cabinet knobs and install them over a window. These items make interesting items to hang curtains from.

- If you have an extra-wide window, use a clothes closet rod (available in home centers) instead of a traditional wooden pole rod. You will enjoy huge savings! Transform these plain rods into custom pieces with paint, fabric, or wallpaper to coordinate with the rest of the room.

- Find a tree branch that is slightly longer than the width of your window. Neaten up the branch by removing any long, scraggly twigs; leave a few branch stubs for character. Leave it natural, or spray paint it to match your decor. Then tie the curtains to the branch following the natural curve of the branch.

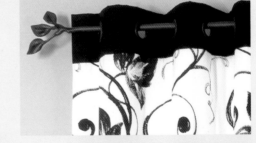

- Paint your existing rods, brackets, and finials to match your new window treatment. It will save you from investing in totally new hardware and can create a stunning finishing touch.

- Finials can be created from many unusual items. I've even used dog chew toys in the shapes of soccer and basketballs in boys' rooms. For unusual curtain finials consider using skateboard wheels, stuffed animals, doorknobs, Christmas ornaments, drawer pulls, feathers, pinecones, artificial flowers, seashells, starfish, or wooden shapes from craft stores.

Every well-dressed bed includes pillow shams — and a color-coordinated cat!

HOME DEC BECK SAYS:

" More than just a place to sleep, your bedroom should be a cozy, dreamy place to relax."

PROJECT 4

Bed Head

QUICK & EASY FLANGED PILLOW SHAMS

This flanged sham is super easy to make and is good for a beginning sewing project. Shams can be easily removed from the pillows because of the overlapping closure on the back. However, you may prefer to keep the shams on at all times and set these pillows aside while you are sleeping. This will certainly save time when making the bed in the morning!

Multiple Choice

Flanged-style pillows are not only for pillow shams. They look just as wonderfully stylish as an accent pillow. Experiment with the width of the flange for different looks.

Round Up

Now, let's get started and gather the following:
– Home dec sewing kit
– $1^5/_8$ yards decorator fabric for each sham
– Thread to match decorator fabric
– Optional, but recommended: $1^5/_8$ yards fleece-type batting for *each* sham
– Optional, but recommended: $1^5/_8$ yards muslin for *each* sham
– Optional: Loose fiberfill

Fabric Swap

Suggested fabrics for this project include drapery-weight cotton, quilt-weight cotton, silk, lightweight chenille and damask.

Go Figure

Need help measuring? Here's where to find it.
– How to Measure Pillows, page 50

On the Cutting Edge

Before cutting into your beautiful fabric, review these cutting tips.
– Cut It Out, page 49
– Fussy Cutting, page 55

Note: If desired, draw a pattern from tissue paper using your cutting dimensions. If making multiple shams, make sure to position the same motif in exactly the same place on each sham.

1. *For a standard-size pillow* (approximately 26 inches by 20 inches): cut the pillow front 33 inches by 27 inches. For the pillow back, cut one rectangle $20^1/_2$ inches by 27 inches and another rectangle $22^1/_2$ inches by 27 inches.

2. *For a queen-size pillow* (approximately 30 inches by 20 inches): cut the pillow front 37 inches by 27 inches. For the pillow back, cut one rectangle $20^1/_2$ inches by 27 inches and another rectangle $26^1/_2$ inches by 27 inches.

3. *For a king-size pillow* (approximately 38 inches by 20 inches): cut the pillow front 44 inches by 27 inches. For the pillow back, cut one rectangle $20^1/_2$ inches by 27 inches and another rectangle $34^1/_2$ inches by 27 inches..

Gearing Up

If you need help setting up your sewing machine, refer to page 42.

PART 3
MAKE IT!

HOME DEC BECK SAYS:

"I like to add additional layers when I make pillow shams — they seem to hold up better and the flanges look crisper. It's really simple to do! Cut a piece of fleece-type batting and a piece of muslin the exact size as the sham front and back pieces. Place the batting on the wrong side of the pillow fabric and top it off with the muslin. Treat this newly created fabric sandwich as one piece of fabric and follow the directions below."

fleece type batting

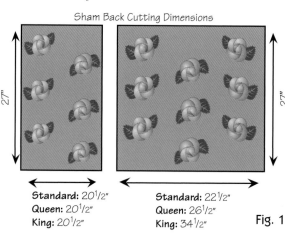
decorator fabric
muslin

"Bed pillows come in standard sizes that are many times indicated on the pillow packaging. However, I have found that the printed measurements are very rarely the same as the actual pillow measurements. They are close, but I usually need to tweak the cutting dimensions slightly. To be sure, measure the length and width of the pillow and add $3\frac{1}{2}$ inches for each flange (a total of 7 inches to the length and width measurement). Compare your measurements to the suggested cutting dimensions below and adjust if needed."

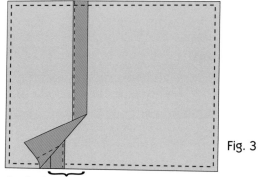

It's Sew Time!

Need to brush up on your sewing skills? Here's where to find help.

– Finishing School, page 52
– Seam Team, page 42
– Go to the Corner, page 43

1. If you are following Beck's advice to make a fabric and batting sandwich, do so now. Otherwise, begin with step 2.

2. Arrange the backing rectangles for hemming as shown in fig. 1.

3. Hem the inside edges of each back rectangle with a double 2-inch hem (fig. 2).

4. With right sides together, pin the sham backs to the sham front so the finished edges of the back pieces overlap as shown (fig. 3). Stitch around all edges of the sham.

5. Trim excess fabric away from the corners.

6. Turn the sham right side out through the opening. With the point turner, go in through the opening and push out the corners to make them as smooth as possible.

Sham Back Cutting Dimensions

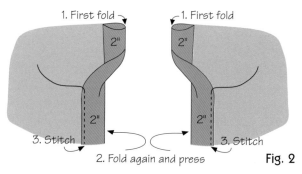

27" 27"

Standard: 20$\frac{1}{2}$"   Standard: 22$\frac{1}{2}$"
Queen: 20$\frac{1}{2}$"   Queen: 26$\frac{1}{2}$"
King: 20$\frac{1}{2}$"   King: 34$\frac{1}{2}$"

Fig. 1

1. First fold   1. First fold
2"   2"
2"   2"
3. Stitch   3. Stitch
2. Fold again and press   Fig. 2

Overlap back until all outside edges are even   Fig. 3

More Splash Than Cash® Decorating Tips

Sooner or later, you will find yourself shopping for a new bed pillow. You'll probably squeeze and fluff the various pillows on the shelf and then quickly realize that you have little or no clue what you are supposed to be looking for. Here are some things to consider when choosing a pillow.

- In general, side sleepers should choose firm pillows, back sleepers should choose medium-firm pillows, and stomach sleepers should opt for soft pillows.

- Pillows made with synthetic fibers or foam are more friendly to allergy-prone people and easy to wash.

- Down pillows are filled with the innermost soft feathers from the breasts of ducks and geese. The fluffiest down comes from geese that live in really cold climates.

- To maintain your pillows, fluff them regularly. This allows the inside of the pillow to absorb fresh air and helps to maintain shape. To fluff, put pillows in a dryer (on the fluff/no heat setting) for 15 minutes with a couple of clean tennis balls.

- Pillows get dirty from daily use. Most synthetic and many down pillows can be washed in a washing machine (check the manufacturer's care instructions). For drying, place them in the dryer with several clean tennis balls, which will aid in the fluffing process.

- If your pillow has a musty smell, set it in the sun for a couple of hours.

- If you have a synthetic pillow and you're trying to determine if you need a new one, try this: Fold it in half and place a shoe on top. If the pillow unfolds and knocks the shoe off, you don't need a new pillow—yet. If the shoe wins, it's time to get a new one.

- For a feather pillow, fold it in half and squeeze out as much air as you can. When you release the pillow, it should unfold on its own. If not, the pillow needs to be replaced.

Fig. 4

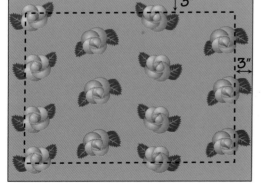

Stitch 3" from edge to create the flange

The Finish Line

To form the flange, topstitch all around the sham 3 inches from the edge (fig. 4).

Compress the pillow and insert the pillow through the opening. Fluff the pillow to fill out the sham

evenly. Arrange the pillow so that it fills all the corners and it is smooth on all sides. If the corners appear empty, put hand fulls of fiber fill into the corners to fill them out.

▶ u dzine it

Since decorating is all about your individual style, here are some ideas for making your own one-of-a-kind pillow sham:

- It's all about the fabric choices. Create your own pillow sham front from assorted scraps by stitching them together in different configurations. Arrange by similar colors or designs.

- Embellish the sham with ribbon and trims.

- Use decorative stitches instead of a traditional straight stitch to stitch the flange seam.

Add color to your walls with these
practical and decorative memo boards.
Minimal sewing is required!

HOME DEC BECK SAYS:

" Don't agonize about being organized."

PROJECT
5

Memo Station

LOW-SEW MEMO BOARDS

9 f you're like me, you have too much stuff and too little time to deal with it. My mail, paperwork, magazines, and appointment cards all create clutter that seem to steal space right out from under my feet! A memo station is an attractive and colorful way to stay organized.

Multiple Choices

This memo station is perfect for keeping us organized, which is key in our busy lives. I have shown two versions in the photo. Either style would be a perfect addition to your office (in or out of the home), right by the door, in the kitchen, in your craft area, or in your kids' rooms — any place you need to keep scattered items together.

Round Up

Now, let's get started and gather the following:
– Home dec sewing kit
– Thread to match decorator fabrics
– Wooden picture frames, each 16 inches
  by 20 inches
– Sturdy cardboard, each 16 inches by 20 inches
– White all-purpose glue
– Decorator fabrics (two coordinating prints
  and an accent fabric)

Memo Station 1 (With One Pocket):

Base fabric and matching pocket: $1^1/_2$ yards
Coordinating pocket: $^1/_2$ yard
Accent fabric on pockek: $^1/_2$ yard
Cork sheet, cut 16 inches by 20 inches (available from art supply stores)

Memo Station 2 (With Three Pockets):

Base fabric and matching pocket: $1^1/_2$ yards
Coordinating pockets: $^1/_2$ yard
Accent fabric on pockets: $^1/_2$ yard

Fabric Swap

Suggested fabrics for this project: 100 percent cotton quilt fabrics

On the Cutting Edge

Before cutting into your beautiful fabric, review these cutting tips.
– Cut It Out, page 49

Memo Station 1

From the base fabric, cut an 18-inch by 22-inch rectangle. From the coordinating fabric, cut one $8^1/_2$inch by 18-inch rectangle for the pocket. From the accent fabric, cut one $9^1/_2$-inch by 18-inch rectangle.

Memo Station 2

From the base fabric, cut an 18-inch by 22-inch rectangle. Also cut an $8^1/_2$-inch by 18-inch rectangle for a pocket. From the coordinating fabric, cut two $8^1/_2$-inch by 18-inch rectangles for the pockets. From the accent fabric, cut three $9^1/_2$-inch by 18-inch rectangles.

Gearing Up

If you need help setting up your sewing machine, refer to page 42.

It's Sew Time!

Need to brush up on your sewing skills? Here's where to find help.
– Seam Team, page 42
– Pressing Matters, page 45

Pocket Construction

Note: All of the pockets for both types of memo boards are made in exactly the same way. Make

PART 3
MAKE IT!

one pocket using the coordinating and accent fabrics for Memo Station 1. Make three pockets for Memo Station 2 (two pockets using the base fabric and one pocket using the coordinating fabric).

1. Place the accent fabric and the pocket fabric right sides together with one 18-inch edge matching. Note: The accent fabric will extend 1 inch below the pocket fabric. Stitch across the top edge with a $1/2$-inch seam allowance (fig. 1).

2. Open the fabric and press the seam allowance toward the accent fabric (fig. 2).

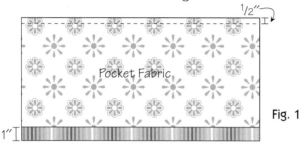

Fig. 1

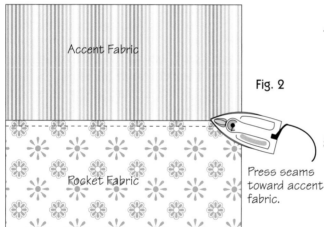

Press seams toward accent fabric.

Fig. 2

3. Fold the pocket so the wrong sides are together and the accent fabric extends $1/2$ inch beyond the pocket fabric. Press smooth. Along the bottom edge of each pocket, stitch a $1/4$-inch seam though both layers of fabric (fig. 3).

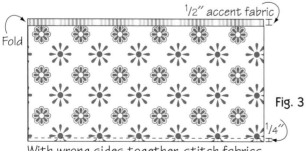

Fig. 3

With wrong sides together, stitch fabrics together $1/4''$ from bottom edge of pocket

Assembly
Memo Station 1

1. Glue the cork sheet to one side of the cardboard.

2. Centering the cork side of the cardboard on the wrong side of the base fabric. (The fabric will extend 1 inch around all four sides). Neatly fold the raw edges of the fabric to the back of the board and glue the fabric in place (fig. 4). Allow the glue to dry.

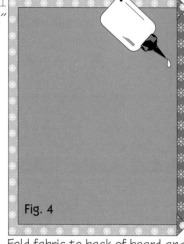

Fig. 4

Fold fabric to back of board and glue all edges

3. Turn the covered board right side up.

4. Place the bottom edge of the pocket even with the bottom edge of the board (fig. 5).

5. Glue the side edges of the pocket to the back of the board.

Fig. 5

Fold excess fabric to back of board and glue in place.

Memo Station 2

1. Center the cardboard on the wrong side of the fabric. (The fabric will extend 1 inch around all four sides). Neatly fold the raw edges of the fabric to the back of the board and glue the fabric in place (refer to fig. 4). Allow the glue to dry.

2. Turn the covered board right side up.

3. Place the first pocket on the board 4 inches down from the top edge. (It will extend 1 inch beyond each side.) Glue each side edge to the back of the board (fig. 6).

4. Place the top edge of the second pocket 4 inches below the first pocket. Glue each side to the back of the board as before.

PART 3
MAKE IT!

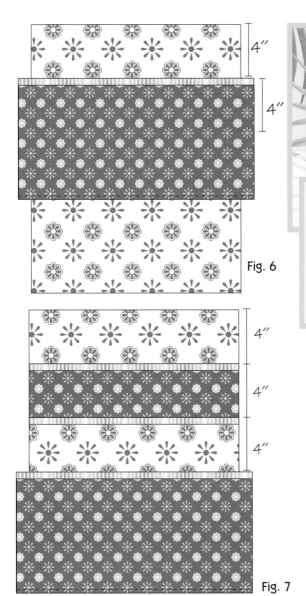

Fig. 6

Fig. 7

Fold excess fabric to back of board and
glue all edges

HOME DEC BECK MINI-PROJECT:

"After creating a unique memo station,
why use boring, plastic pushpins?"

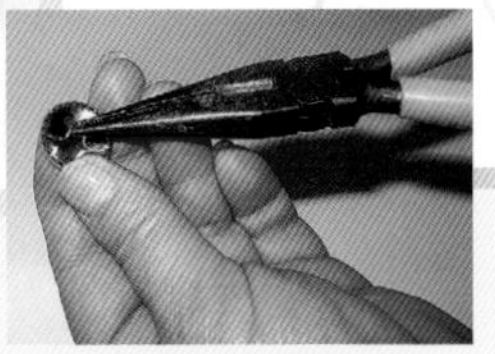

Fancy Schmancy Pushpins

All you need to do to make your own is
to cover $^5/_8$-inch-diameter button forms with fabric (if the
backing has a small loop on the back, remove it first with
pliers). Then, using your hot glue gun, glue pushpins or
quilter's thumbtacks onto the back of the fabric-covered
buttons. Now, how cute are they?

▶ u dzine it

Since decorating is all about your individual style,
here are some ideas on how to make your one-of-
a-kind memo station:

- Use a vintage frame instead of a sleek, purchased one.

- Make your own frame with wood molding found
at the home improvement store.

- Create memo stations in different sizes and
shapes.

5. Place the top edge of the third pocket 4 inches
below the second pocket (fig. 7). The bottom
edge of this pocket should be even with the
bottom edge of the board. Glue each side of the
pocket to the back of the board.

The Finish Line

Remove the glass from the picture frame. You
won't need it for this project. Place the fabric
covered cardboard into the frame. Secure the
board in place with the metal tabs on the back
of the frame. If the picture frame came with a
cardboard backing, place it on top of the memo
board before securing the tabs. Hang on wall
where desired.

More Splash Than Cash® Decorating Tips

A home can never have enough places to
store stuff. Consider these suggestions for
some super storage solutions:

- Stack graduated sizes of suitcases and use
them as a bedside table. Fill the suitcases
with seldom-used treasures.

- Install shelving about 10 to 12 inches
below the ceiling in a hallway and store
your books and collectibles on it.

- Create your own instant storage space with
a (clean!) plastic garbage can and a round
piece of wood. Use the garbage can as the
base and the round piece of wood as the
top. Fill the garbage can with seasonal
items (for example sweaters or holiday
ornaments). Disguise the "table" by covering it with a floor-length round table cloth.

PART 3
MAKE IT!

An ottoman is the perfect surface for fireside entertaining.

HOME DEC BECK SAYS:

" This is one thing I know for sure. When your cat has fallen asleep in your lap and is totally content and utterly adorable, you will suddenly have to pee."

PROJECT 6

Lounge Act

BUILD AN OTTOMAN FROM START TO FINISH

W hat a great piece of furniture! An ottoman can perform double duty in your home as a coffee table or extra seating when you need it. And you won't hear the words "Take your feet off the furniture" because that's what an ottoman is made for!

Multiple Choices

The basic upholstery techniques used for this project can easily be adapted to cover a chair seat, the lid of a clothes hamper, a barstool, or even an upholstered headboard.

Round Up

Now, let's get started and gather the following:

From the Fabric Store

– Home dec sewing kit
– Decorator fabric, $1^1/_2$ yards of 54-inch-wide fabric
– Thread to match decorator fabric
– One 30-inch circle cut from 4-inch-thick high-density foam (If you can't find 4-inch-thick foam, create the height with layers of 2-inch foam and glue them together just like a layer cake.)
– Special spray adhesive for foam (don't use regular spray adhesive as it might damage the foam)
– $1^1/_2$ yards of extra-thick upholstery batting (the type purchased off a roll — not in a precut package)
– 29-inch circle of felt
– Fabric glue
– Staple gun and staples
– Spray foam glue

From the Home Improvement Store

– 30-inch wooden round (cut from $1/_2$-inch plywood)
– Four, 12-inch coffee table legs

Fabric Swap

For this project use any sturdy fabric of your choice including upholstery fabric, tapestry, denim, and canvas.

On the Cutting Edge

Before cutting into your beautiful fabric, review these cutting tips.
– Cut It Out, page 49

1. Straighten one end of the fabric. Cut two strips of fabric, each 7 inches wide by the width of the fabric. Measure the circumference of your wooden circle. (It should be approximately 95 inches.) Cut the strips so that when stitched together they will equal the circumference measurement of the wooden circle. Set aside. These are the band strips.

2. Cut a 31-inch circle from the fabric for the ottoman top. To do this, fold the fabric into quarters and pin the layers together so they won't shift as you cut. The center of the circle is the corner where all the folds meet. Secure one end of a tape measure to the center point with a pushpin. Measure $15^1/_2$ inches from the center point and, using the tape

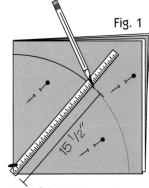

Fig. 1

15 1/2"

Fold fabric into quarters and tack tape measure at folded center point

HOME DEC BECK SAYS:

"I cut a 30-inch plywood circle using my handy jigsaw and found the coffee table legs on the Internet. To cut the upholstery foam into a circle you'll need an electric carving knife (you know, the kind used to carve turkeys on Thanksgiving). Or, ask an upholstery shop to cut a circle for you."

as a compass, draw a quarter circle with a fabric marker (fig. 1). Cut along the drawn line.

3. Use the wood circle as a template and trace around the shape onto the foam. Carefully cut the foam circle with an electric carving knife.

Gearing Up

If you need help setting up your sewing machine, refer to page 42.

It's Sew Time!

Need to brush up on your sewing skills? Here's where to find help.
– Seam Team, page 42
– Pressing Matters, page 45

1. To make the band, place the two strips right sides together and stitch both ends, forming a large circle. Press the seams open (fig. 2). Divide the band and the top circle into four equal sections. Place a pin at each mark (figs. 2 and 3).

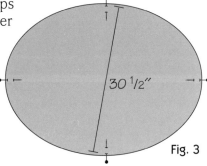

Fig. 2

Fig. 3

Pinmark the ottoman circle top at each quartermark

30 1/2"

2. Place the band and the top circle right sides together, matching the quarter markings on the band to the quarter markings on the circle.

Then pin the remaining sections of the circle and band together.

3. Stitch the band to the top circle (fig. 4).

The Finish Line

Work in a well-ventilated area when using spray adhesive. Protect the work surface from the adhesive with paper or an old sheet.

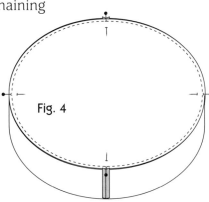

Fig. 4

With right sides together, stitch the band to the circle, matching quarter marks. Use additional pins as needed to hold layers in place.

1. Place the wood circle on a large work surface. Spray the wood surface lightly with the foam adhesive. Also spray one side of the high-density foam with the adhesive. Place the adhesive sides together and apply pressure so the two layers adhere to one another (fig. 5).

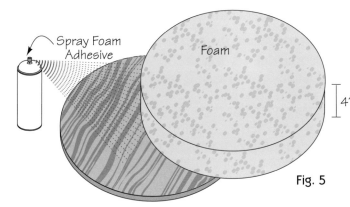

Spray Foam Adhesive

Foam

4"

Fig. 5

Spray the wood surface and one side of the foam with adhesive, then place sprayed sides together and apply pressure

2. Place the batting on the surface and center the ottoman top, foam side down, over the batting. Bring one edge of the batting to the wood circle and staple 1 inch in from the edge. Directly opposite this staple, do the same thing. Repeat at remaining two quarter side points.

3. Continue stapling the batting to the wood (fig. 6). Trim excess batting as necessary to make this process less cumbersome.

 PART 3 MAKE IT!

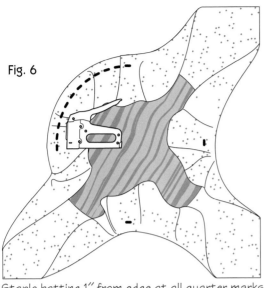

Fig. 6

Staple batting 1″ from edge at all quarter marks to back of ottoman top

Felt

Fig. 8

4. On a clean surface, place the fabric cover wrong side up. Insert the ottoman top, foam side down, into the opening. The cover should be really snug. You want it to fit like a glove over the ottoman top.

5. Now the fun begins! Work the ottoman top into the cover until it fills out the top. This step is much like squeezing into your favorite tight jeans. Do what you have to do to make this happen. Be persistent – it will work.

6. Turn the ottoman top over and make sure the fabric is smooth over the top and sides. Then turn it back over and secure the fabric to the wood like you did the batting. Pull the fabric taut as you do this to keep it smooth. Trim any excess fabric for a neat finish (fig. 7)

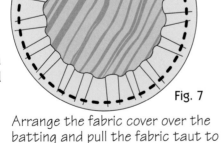

Fig. 7

Arrange the fabric cover over the batting and pull the fabric taut to the back and staple along the edge.

7. Glue or staple the felt circle on the wrong side of the ottoman top to cover all the raw edges of the ottoman cover.

8. Decide on placement of the legs (they should form a square). Following the package direc-

tions for the legs, screw them into the wood (fig. 8).

▶ **u dzine it**

Since decorating is all about your individual style, here are some ideas on how to make your one-of-a-kind ottoman:

• Glue a luxurious fringe trim to the edge of the wood base.

• Use a wooden spool (that electric wire comes on) as the ottoman base.

• Other creative ottoman bases could be a barrel-shaped flower planter, a wine crate, a cabinet drawer, a plant stand, or even a suitcase.

• Instead of furniture legs, use fence posts or curtain finials.

• Add contrasting cording in the seam that connects the top circle to the side band.

• Give the ottoman a studly look with decorative upholstery studs.

• Cut fabric into four equal wedges, then stitch them together to form a circle and use it as the ottoman cover. This can be especially effective with stripes or fabrics with a nap.

• Don't stop at a circle as an ottoman base. Cut the wooden base into a square, a rectangle a boomerang or kidney shapes.

The same upholstery techniques used to make the ottoman can be used to cover chair seats.

Have friends over. Take off your shoes. Warm up the room without touching the thermostat with a beautiful throw you made yourself.

HOME DEC BECK SAYS:

"When I come home after a busy day, I like to do nothing. And then rest afterward."

PROJECT 7

Rest Assured

LEARN TO SEW A DECORATIVE THROW 2 STYLES

𝓘 love a fabric throw! And almost any place you look for decorating advice, you will find the suggestion to add one to your room. Not only are they a key decorating accessory, they also have a practical side. A throw keeps you warm as you're reading a book, catching a snooze, snuggling with a furry friend, or watching TV. And, of course, they can be strategically placed to cover a worn or stained spot on your furniture!

A perfect throw is hard to find – that is, one in the right color *and* at the right price. So making one is the natural solution. My friend, Victoria Waller, told me about a throw she made with jacquard fabric and trim. I thought her idea was so great that I had to share it with you. The basic throw is easy to sew. If you are up to a slight challenge, add some fun trim (I've included instructions for both). This is a great project for gifts, too!

Multiple Choices

Drape a throw over the aforementioned chair or sofa, but don't forget the ottoman, bench, and your bed. Don't take the arrangement of it too seriously. After all, it is not called a throw for nothing. Grab one end and let it drape nonchalantly on the furniture, or grab the center and toss it casually over a chair.

Use these same sewing techniques to make a square or rectangular tablecloth (only stitch the double hem toward the wrong side and omit the trim). Napkins can also be made using this technique; only use a double $^1/_2$ inch hem.

Fabric Swap

A fabric that looks good on both sides is the key to success for this project. Any fabric with a woven

(not printed) pattern or design is a good choice for this project including jacquard, damask, tapestry, wool and silk dupioni. This information will help you choose the right fabric.

– Knowing Right from Wrong, page 48
– Prep School, page 47

Round Up

Now, let's get started and gather the following:
– Home dec sewing kit
– 2 yards of 54"-wide reversible fabric
– Thread to match decorator fabric
Optional: Ball fringe, $6^1/_2$ yards

On the Cutting Edge

Before you cut into your beautiful fabric, review these cutting tips.
– Let's Get This Straight, page 53
– Cut It Out, page 49

1. Straighten both cut edges of the fabric.

2. Trim the selvages evenly from each side of the fabric.

3. The cut size should be *approximately* 53 inches by 70 inches.

Gearing Up

If you need help setting up your sewing machine, refer to page 42.

PART 3 MAKE IT!

along the innermost intersection of the fold lines and press (fig. 3). Unfold. Then create a new fold across the outermost intersection of the fold lines and press. Cut off the fabric at this new diagonal line (fig. 4). Refold the hems, (fig. 5). The hems will meet at a 45-degree angle and form a mitered corner (fig. 6).

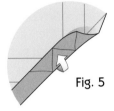

Fig. 3

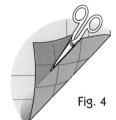

Fig. 4

Fig. 5

Refold on original hem lines

Fig. 6

It's Sew Time!

Need to brush up on your sewing skills? Here's where to find help.
Pressing Matters, page 45
The Bottom Line, page 44
Finishing School, page 52
Cinch of a Stitch, page 45

Basic Throw

1. Determine what side of the fabric you want as the right side. Lay the fabric with your chosen side up.

2. Fold and press a double 2-inch hem along the top and bottom edges. Do not stitch. Then fold and press a double 2-inch hem along the side edges (fig. 1). Do not stitch.

3. Working one corner at a time, open the pressed hems. You will see criss-crossed fold lines in the corner area (fig. 2).

4. To miter the corner, diagonally fold the point

5. Handstitch the diagonal edges closed at each mitered corner (fig. 7). Do not stitch through to the back of the throw; the entire double hem should remain open.

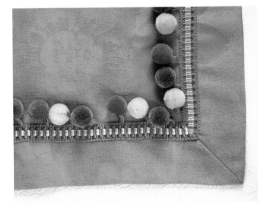

2"

2"

Fig. 7

6. Go to "The Finish Line"

The Finish Line

With Trim

If you are applying the trim to the surface as shown in the photo, center the trim on the folded hem edge. Stitch along each edge of the trim, one side at a time. Stitch the outside edge first, then the inside edge. Stop stitching at the folded hem edge of the adjoining corner (fig. 8). Fold the trim

Fig. 1

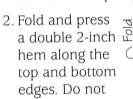

Fold

Fold

Fold

Fold

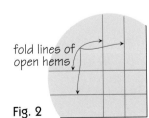

fold lines of open hems

Fig. 2

PART 3
MAKE IT!

HOME DEC BECK SAYS:

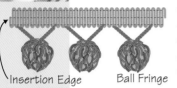

"Trims are designed to be attached to fabric in one of two ways — into the seams as you construct your project or directly on the surface. Most trims are constructed with two components: an insertion edge and a decorative edge. The insertion edge is really just the trim's seam allowance.

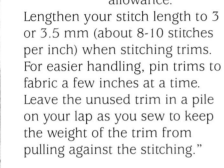

Insertion Edge   Ball Fringe

Lengthen your stitch length to 3 or 3.5 mm (about 8-10 stitches per inch) when stitching trims. For easier handling, pin trims to fabric a few inches at a time. Leave the unused trim in a pile on your lap as you sew to keep the weight of the trim from pulling against the stitching."

back over itself and stitch a 45 degree seam line through the trim and throw (fig. 9). Then arrange the trim so it covers the inside miter fold and lies flat on the perpendicular side. Continue stitching along the outside edge of the trim, followed with stitching along inside edge of trim (fig. 10).

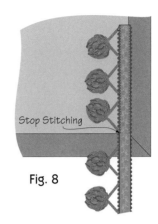

Stop Stitching

Fig. 8

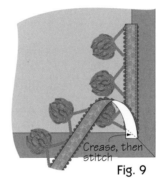

Crease, then stitch

Fig. 9

Fig. 10

More Splash Than Cash® Decorating Tips

Mix, match, and mingle fabric to your heart's content! Part of the fun in decorating is to pick great fabrics and think of creative ways to use them.

- Cover the simple lines of several picture frames with fabric for fun accessories.
- Cover an otherwise unattractive table with a floor-length table skirt. Add a lavish topper for an outstanding look.
- Add a colorful mantel scarf to make your fireplace a colorful focal point in a room.
- Fabric-covered walls are an interesting way to soften a room.
- Cover the inside of a freestanding bookshelf with fabric that coordinates with the room.
- Transform a plain white lampshade into something special by covering the shade with fabric.

Without Trim

If you are not adding trim, secure the folded hem to the throw fabric with pins. Carefully stitch close to the fold to hold the hem in place (fig. 11). Don't forget to remove the pins along the way. You're done!

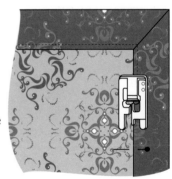

Fig. 11

▶ u dzine it

Since decorating is all about your individual style, here are some ideas for making your one-of-a-kind throw:

- Gather men's wool sport coats. Cut them up into even-size squares. Stitch the squares together in a pleasing pattern to form the front of the throw. Add a backing (like a pillow) and enjoy!
- Stitch two rectangles of fabric around all four edges and turn the piece right side out like a pillow. With contrasting thread, stitch a planned pattern (such as squares or diamonds) or a freeform design through both layers to decorate.

PART 3
MAKE IT!

It's hard to beat the simplicity of design and style, much less the easy sewing techniques, of this window treatment.

HOME DEC BECK SAYS:

"All kittens think that curtains are for climbing."

Say ta-ta to ho-hum window treatments! These curtains are so stylish your friends will scream with envy when they see them in your home. This simple window treatment is threaded onto the curtain rod through the large fashion-forward grommets. The fabric automatically arranges itself into soft, gorgeous folds. The grommets glide smoothly over the rod so the curtain can be easily opened or closed. The grommets are easy to insert into the fabric — no special equipment is needed! They come in a variety of colors and just simply snap together. They also unsnap and can be reused in a future project.

Multiple Choices

Don't think of curtains as being just for windows! You can use these same directions and make a curtain to use as a closet "door," a shower curtain, or a room divider. Using a tension rod, curtains can also substitute for cabinet doors in your bathroom or kitchen. Hang curtains on the wall behind your bed (with or without a headboard) to add instant height or additional color to your room. If you make this curtain style shorter, it becomes a café curtain or, shorter yet, a valance.

Curtain grommets are available in different sizes and colors.

Round Up

Now, let's get started and gather the following:
– Home dec sewing kit

– Decorator fabric for the curtain*
– Coordinating fabric for the upper cuff (only if you are making version 1)*
– Lining fabric*
– Thread to match decorator and lining fabrics
– Decorative rod (no larger than $1\frac{3}{8}$-inch diameter), mounting brackets, and finials
– Large grommets, $1\frac{9}{16}$-inch diameter (an even number for each curtain panel)
*Calculated to fit your window.

Fabric Swap

Suggested fabrics for this project include drapery-weight cotton fabric, quilt-weight cotton fabric, linen, silk, or jacquard.

Go Figure

Need help measuring? Here's where to find it.
How to Measure a Window, page 50
Support System, page 58
The Right Height, page 58

Version 1: No contrasting cuff

1. Mount the rod above the window. Measure from the top edge of the rod to the desired finished length (fig. 1). That's measurement A: ___.

2. Add $10\frac{1}{2}$ inches and that's measurement B: ___. This is your cut-length measurement.

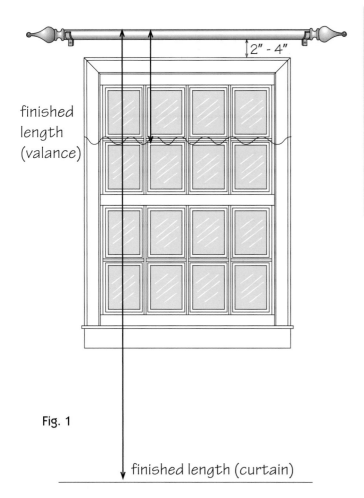

finished length (valance)

2" - 4"

Fig. 1

finished length (curtain)

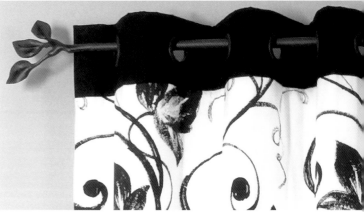

Like a sweep of eyeliner, the black border in this curtain makes magic on this version of a grommet curtain.

Version 2: Curtain with coordinating upper cuff
Lower Section (Curtain)

1. Mount the rod above the window. Measure from the top edge of the curtain rod to the desired finished length. That's measurement A: ___.

2. Add $4^1/_2$ inches and that's measurement B: ___. This is your cut-length measurement for the lower section curtain fabric.

3. Continue with steps 3 through 9 from Version 1.

Cuff

Multiply (E) by 6 inches and divide by 36 inches for the total yardage needed for the cuff: ___.

Lining (both versions)

1. Measure from the top edge of the curtain rod to the desired finished length. Add $7^1/_2$ inches to get BB: ___. This is the cut-length measurement for the lining.

2. Multiply BB by E (determined in step 5 of Version 1): ___.

3. Finally, divide by 36 inches for the total yardage needed for the lining fabric: ___.

On the Cutting Edge

Before cutting into your beautiful fabric, review these cutting tips.

3. Measure the distance between the brackets and multiply this number by $1^1/_2$ or 2 (depending on how full you want the curtain to be). That's measurement C: ___.

4. The width of your fabric is measurement D: ___.

5. Divide (C) by (D). Round up to the nearest whole number to get measurement E: ___. This is the number of fabric widths you need to cut.

6. The fabric's repeat distance (if applicable) is measurement F: ___.

7. Add (B) and (F) and that's measurement G: ___.

8. Multiply (G) by (E) and that's measurement H: ___.

9. Divide (H) by 36 inches for the total yardage needed for the decorator fabric for the lower section.

More Splash Than Cash

PART 3
MAKE IT!

Fabric for curtain (versions 1 and 2)

Straighten one end of the fabric. Cut one fabric width to the cut-length measurement (B). Using this width as a guide, cut additional fabric widths (E). Don't forget to match the design repeats as you cut the additional fabric widths.

Cuff (version 1 only)

1. Straighten one end of the fabric. Cut one fabric width 6-inches wide.

2. Cut the same number of cuff strips as you did for the bottom section (E).

Lining (for versions 1 and 2)

1. Straighten one end of the lining fabric. Cut one fabric width to the cut-length measurement (BB).

2. Cut additional fabric widths (E).

Gearing Up

If you need help setting up your sewing machine, refer to page 42.

It's Sew Time!

Need to brush up on your sewing skills? Here's where to find help.
– Seam Team, page 42

– Pressing Matters, page 45
– Split Personality, page 56
– Matchmaking, page 57
– Lining Up, page 52
– Finishing School, page 52
– The Bottom Line, page 44

Version 1 (without cuff)

Divide the decorator fabric widths to create two curtain panels according to the number of widths you cut. Then sew the widths right sides together to create separate panels; match repeats if necessary. Finish seams as desired (use a zigzag stitch or pink the raw edges). Press the seams open.

Version 2 (with cuff)

1. For the lower section, divide the decorator fabric widths to create two curtain panels according to the number of widths you cut. Then sew the widths right sides together to create separate panels; match repeats if necessary. Finish seams as desired (use a zigzag stitch or pink the raw edges). Press the seams open.

2. In the same manner, cut and stitch the cuff strips together, short end to short end. Finish the seams as desired (use a zigzag stitch or pink the raw edges). Press the seams open.

More Splash Than Cash® Decorating Tips

It's understandable that you would like to be able to throw your curtains in your washer and dryer for easy cleaning. But think about this for a minute. You have invested your time and effort into creating the perfect window treatment, and your hard work may literally go down the drain if you wash your project. Your window treatment will lose it's body if it is washed. Instead, keep your window treatments clean and fresh looking by following these tips:

• Always work with clean hands during the construction process.

• Regularly vacuum your window treatments to remove dust and pollen. Pay particular attention to pleats and gathers where dust gathers.

• Hang your window treatments outside on a dry slightly breezy day to freshen them. Alternatively, place a curtain panel and a damp—not wet—cloth into the dryer. Turn the dryer on "air fluff" (no heat) and tumble for about 15 minutes. The tumbling action shakes the dirt and dust free, and the cloth absorbs these impurities.

• If the window treatments in the same room are the same size, rotate them periodically from window to window. Because different windows get different sun exposure, this prevents one treatment from wearing out or fading before another.

**PART 3
MAKE IT!**

3. Stitch the cuff to the top edge of the lower section (fig. 2). Press both seams toward the lower section of the curtain panel. Treat this unit now as one piece of fabric.

Both Versions

1. Stitch the lining fabric widths together. Then trim the lining fabric so it is 6 inches narrower and 3 inches shorter than each curtain panel.

2. Hem the bottom edge of each lining panel with a double 3-inch hem.

3. Hem the bottom edge of each curtain panel with a double 4-inch hem.

4. Center the lining over the curtain panel right sides together. The curtain panel should extend 3 inches beyond the left and right side edges of the lining. Pin, making sure the top edges of the decorator and lining fabrics are even and the bottom edge of the lining is 1 inch shorter than the curtain panel. Stitch the fabrics together along the top edge (fig. 3).

5. Bring the lining over to the wrong side of the curtain. Press the top edge smooth, including the remaining $1/2$ inch top seam allowance that extends on each side of the lining (fig. 4). Stitch close to the top edge through all layers to prevent the lining from showing on the right side.

6. Hem the side edges of each curtain panel with a double $1^1/2$-inch hem, encasing the lining into the hem (fig. 5).

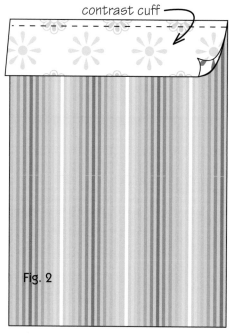

contrast cuff

Fig. 2

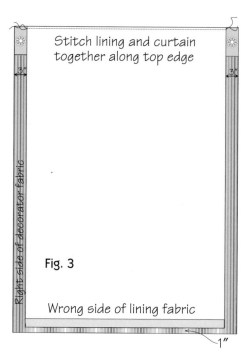

Stitch lining and curtain together along top edge

3"

3"

Right side of decorator fabric

Fig. 3

Wrong side of lining fabric

1"

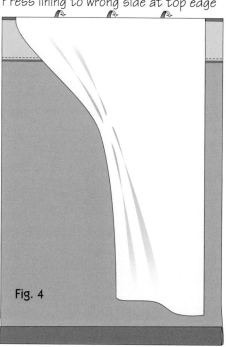

Press lining to wrong side at top edge

Fig. 4

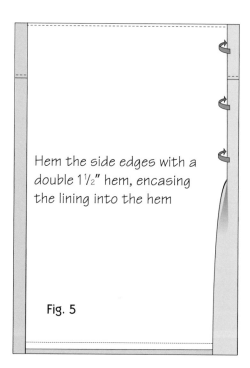

Hem the side edges with a double $1^1/2$" hem, encasing the lining into the hem

Fig. 5

The Finish Line

1. On the lining, draw a line across the full width of the curtain $2^1/2$ inches from the top finished edge.

2. Plan the placement of the grommets. The centers of the first and last grommet should be 2 inches from each side edge. Divide the remaining area evenly for the number of grom-

PART 3 MAKE IT!

A valance is made exactly like a floor-length curtain, only it is shorter.

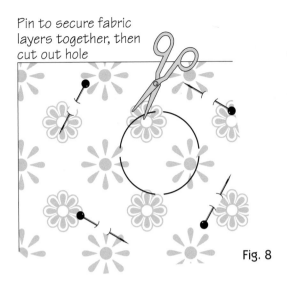

Pin to secure fabric layers together, then cut out hole

Fig. 8

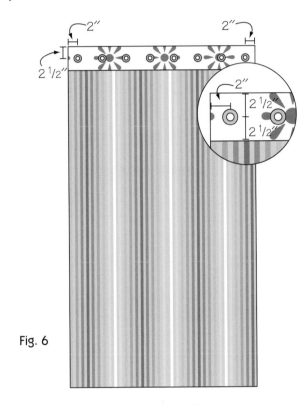

Fig. 6

mets you are using (fig. 6). Always use an even number of grommets.

3. Position the grommet template (included in the grommet package), on the drawn line and trace the slots (fig. 7) at each grommet mark. Pin around the mark so the fabric does not shift. Cut out the grommet circle (fig. 8). Follow the package directions to insert the grommets.

Trace in slots to mark grommet   Fig. 7

Template for 1 9/16" Curtain Grommet

4. Insert the rod through the grommets.

5. Attach the rod to the brackets.

6. With your hands, arrange your curtains into attractive folds.

▶ u dzine it

Since decorating is all about your individual style, here are some ideas on how to make your one-of-a-kind grommet curtain. Grommets don't have to be functional; they can also be decorative. Consider these ideas, or come up with some of your own.

• Add evenly spaced grommets to the remaining three sides of the curtain.

• Create a design within the interior of the curtain panel with the grommets. Scatter them over the entire curtain for a peek-a-boo effect.

• Cut circles (using the grommet as a pattern) from different colored or sheer fabrics and glue them to the wrong side of the decorative grommet after they have been inserted in the curtain.

• Grommets come in different colors. Use a mix of colors on the same curtain.

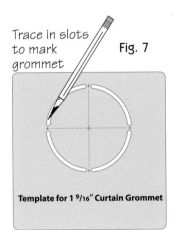

HOME DEC BECK SAYS:

"After a long day of sewing, schedule a massage. You deserve it!"

PART 3
MAKE IT!

Whether or not you want to curl up with a good book or completely sack out, your bedroom should not scimp on comfort or style.

Fabric for duvet cover courtesy of Robert Allen @ Home

PROJECT 9 | Comfort Zone

EASY TO SEW DUVET COVER

Think of those long, lazy weekend mornings when you get to turn off the alarm clock, pull the covers up, and hunker down in delicious slumber to enjoy a few more minutes of sleep. This image brings to mind a soft, cushy comforter to wrap you in a protective cocoon.

Thank goodness you don't have to wait for weekends to enjoy a luxurious bed to fall asleep in. A few hours of sewing and beautiful fabric are all you need to create a duvet cover that will transform your bed into a heavenly place every day of the week!

A duvet cover (also known as a comforter cover) is a practical and decorative way to cover a feather, down, or synthetic-filled comforter. It is easy to make—just think of it as an extra-large pillowcase!

Multiple Choices

Adapt these instructions to make a futon mattress cover or even a summer-weight sleeping bag for your kids.

Round Up

Now, let's get started and gather the following:
– Home dec sewing kit
– Decorator fabric (If you plan to use your duvet cover in lieu of a top sheet, choose a fabric that feels good against your skin – especially for the lining side of the cover. Also, make sure the fabrics you select are washable.)
– Thread to match the background color of the fabric
– $5^1/_2$ yards twill tape
– $^1/_2$ yard fusible hook-and-loop tape

Fabric Swap

Suggested fabrics for this project include: chenille, damask, matelasse, quilt-weight cotton fabrics, flannel, and drapery-weight cotton fabrics.

Go Figure

Need help measuring? Here's where to find it.
– How to Measure a Duvet Cover, page 50

1. For the duvet front, measure the length of your duvet. Add 17 $^1/_2$ inches and that's measurement A: ___. This is your cut-length measurement for the front.

2. For the duvet back, measure the length of your duvet. Subtract $2^1/_2$ inches and that's measurement B: ___. This is your cut-length measurement for the back.

3. Measure the width of your duvet and add 7 inches. That's measurement C: ___. This is your cut width measurement for both the front and the back.

4. The fabric width is measurement D: ___.

5. Divide (C) by (D). Round up to the nearest whole number and that's measurement E: ___.

PART 3
MAKE IT!

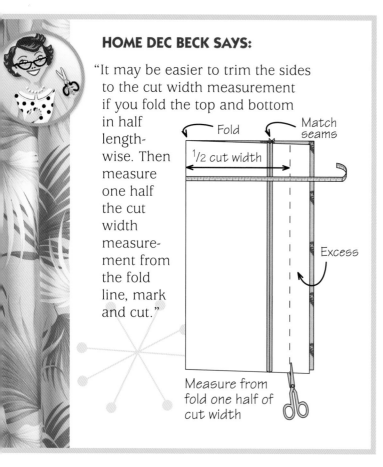

HOME DEC BECK SAYS:

"It may be easier to trim the sides to the cut width measurement if you fold the top and bottom in half lengthwise. Then measure one half the cut width measurement from the fold line, mark and cut."

Fold

Match seams

1/2 cut width

Excess

Measure from fold one half of cut width

This is the number of fabric widths you need per side of the duvet cover. (If you're making a reversible cover, you'll need to cut one set of fabric widths from each fabric.)

6. The fabric's repeat distance (if applicable) is measurement F: ___.

7. Add (A) and (F) together ___. Then multiply total by (E) to get measurement G: ___.

8. Add (B) and (F) together ___. Then multiply total by (E) to get measurement H: ___.

9. Add (G) and (H) together and divide by 36 inches for the total yardage you need: ___.

On the Cutting Edge

Before cutting into your beautiful fabric, review these cutting tips.
– Let's Get This Straight, page 53
– Worth Repeating, page 54
– Fussy Cutting, page 55
– Repeat after Me, page 54
– The Great Divide, page 55
– Cut It Out, page 49

1. Straighten one end of the fabric. Cut one width of fabric to the cut length measurement A.

2. Using this width as a guide, cut additional widths you need (E) for the duvet front. Don't forget to match the design repeats as you cut the additional fabric widths.

3. Using B as the cut-length measurement, repeat steps 1 and 2 to cut the back fabric widths.

Gearing Up

If you need help setting up your sewing machine, refer to page 42.

It's Sew Time!

Need to brush up on your sewing skills? Here's where to find help.
– Seam Team, page 42
– Pressing Matters, page 45
– Split Personality, page 56
– Matchmaking, page 57
– Finishing School, page 52
– Cutting It Down To Size, page 57
– Go To The Corner, page 43

1. For the front of the cover, sew the fabric pieces right sides together; match repeats if necessary. Finish seam edges as desired (use a zigzag stitch, pink the raw edges, or make French seams). Press the seams open unless using French seams. Repeat for the back.

2. Trim the side edges evenly to the cut width measurement (C).

3. Repeat for the duvet cover back.

4. Along the top edges of the cover front and back, fold over and press a double 2-inch hem toward the wrong side. Stitch along the folded edge (fig. 1).

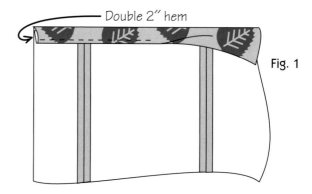

Double 2″ hem

Fig. 1

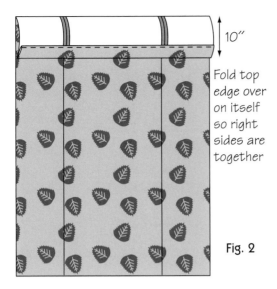

10"

Fold top
edge over
on itself
so right
sides are
together

Fig. 2

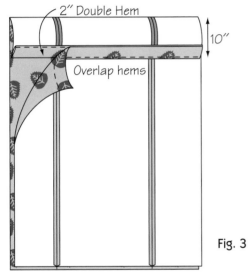

2" Double Hem

Overlap hems

10"

Fig. 3

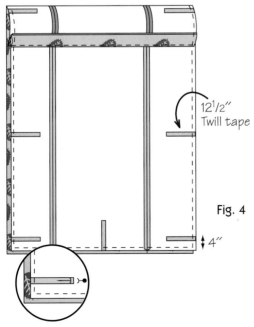

12½"
Twill tape

Fig. 4

4"

HOME DEC BECK SAYS:

" No day is so bad that it
can't be cured with a nap.
So, cuddle up!"

5. Lay the cover front right side up on your work surface. Fold the finished top edge down 10 inches so the right sides are together (fig. 2)

6. Now pin the back and the front with right sides together overlapping the double hems. Match the two side edges and the bottom edge (fig. 3).

7. Cut twill tape into seven, 12½ inch lengths for the ties. Pin the ties 4 inches up from each bottom corner, in the middle of each side, and in the two corners. Arrange the ties so they are perpendicular to the edge and pin in place. Stitch around three sides as shown (fig. 4). Note: You can add more ties to the cover if you want.

8. Turn the cover right side out. Arrange it on a large surface so it is smooth and flat. Press seams carefully so that no fabric is visible from the opposite side.

9. To create the flange, use a fabric marker and mark 3 inches from the edge along both sides and the bottom. Beginning at the right upper corner, stitch directly on this line around the cover, catching only the ends of the ties in the stitching (fig. 5).

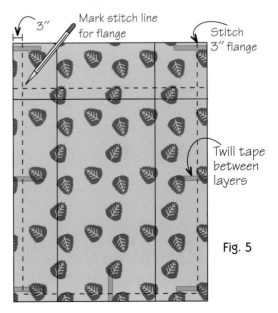

3" Mark stitch line for flange Stitch 3" flange

Twill tape between layers

Fig. 5

PART 3 MAKE IT!

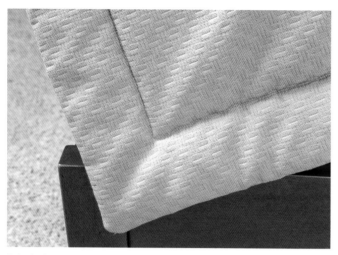

Stitch 3 inches from edge to create a decorative flange.

The Finish Line

1. Cut the fusible hook-and-loop tape into 5-inch-lengths. Keeping the hook and loop sections together, arrange them so they are evenly spaced between the openings of the cover on the hemmed sections (fig. 6). Following manufacturer's instructions, fuse the tape to the cover.

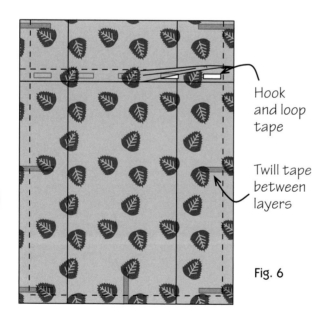

Hook and loop tape

Twill tape between layers

Fig. 6

2. Cut left over twill tape into seven, 9-inch lengths for the ties. Stitch these ties to the duvet at each corner and in the middle of each side and bottom to correspond to the tie positions inside the cover (fig. 7). Note: If you added more ties to your cover, don't forget to add additional ties to the duvet.

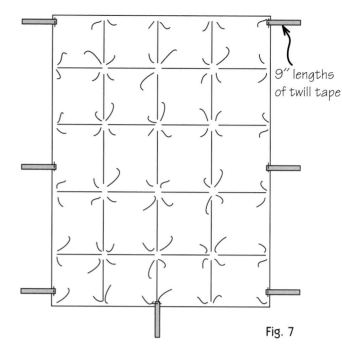

9" lengths of twill tape

Fig. 7

3. Roll your duvet into a tight roll. Open the cover and place the duvet inside the cover and tie the bottom ties of the duvet and the cover together. Unroll the cover, tie the middle side ties, and finish with the top corner ties.

▶ u dzine it

Since decorating is all about your individual style, here are some ideas for making your one-of-a-kind duvet cover:

- Use one fabric for the center panel and a coordinating fabric for the side panels.

- Randomly stitch a bunch of fabric squares together to use as the cover front.

- Instead of piecing the fabric widths vertically as in the instructions stitch the fabric widths so they lie horizontally across the bed.

HOME DEC BECK SAYS:

" Consider making the duvet reversible for an easy seasonal change. Choose a dark-colored fabric for one side and a light colored fabric for the other. Make two sets of pillow shams, one in each of the two fabrics, to complete a seasonal transformation."

PART 3
MAKE IT!

More Splash Than Cash® Decorating Tips

When decorating your bedroom, indulge your-self with luxury. sight, sound, touch, and smell should all be considered when creating a personal retreat.

- Do you know what makes sleeping in a hotel bed so sexy? (Hint: it's not the chocolate on the pillow.) It's the easy-to-slide-between sheets. A new set for your bed will do wonders, setting the stage for a comfortable (and romantic) haven. The magic words when shopping for sheets are "thread count" and you are looking for nothing less than 250.

- If your bedroom window provides a wonderful view, arrange your bed so that you can look out your window first thing in the morning.

- An easy-to-make and budget-friendly Roman shade is a stylish window treatment for bed-rooms. The shade provides both privacy and a layer of insulation. It also pairs well with floor-length curtains. You'll find complete instruc-tions for these projects on page 113 (Roman shade) and pages 79 and 101 for floor-length curtains.

- A fresh coat of paint is a quick, easy, and an affordable decorating project. Consider painting the wall behind your bed a color to show off your new duvet cover!

- When making your bed, fold the duvet cover back to expose coordinating blanket and sheets underneath. This inviting arrangement adds subtle texture to the room. Another easy way to add texture to your bedroom décor is to casu-ally toss a throw at the foot of your bed. You'll find instructions for an easy throw on page 97.

- Add a plush area rug beside your bed to keep your tootsies warm on a cold winter night.

- Replace your stuffed animal collection (if you haven't already!) with a profusion of comfy and stylish pillows. Rearrange them when you want a different look. Mix and match fabrics, shapes, and sizes when piling on this layer of luxury. Instructions for pillows and pillow shams are on pages 65 and 85.

Mix and match the projects in this book to create your dream bedroom.

Roman shades are unfussy and require only a minimum amount of fabric. It's the perfect budget-friendly choice for window treatments.

HOME DEC BECK SAYS:

"I have made lots of Roman shades. This is absolutely, positively the easiest method I have used. Don't be intimidated by the number of steps. This project is really quite easy to sew."

PROJECT

10 | Shade Simplicity

SIMPLE TO SEW ROMAN SHADE

When deciding on a window treatment, it's hard to ignore a sure thing. And when one window treatment is the answer to so many situations, it's no wonder that the Roman shade is such a popular choice. This easy-to-make and budget-friendly window treatment combines functionality with simple design. This stylish shade is a chameleon — it works for most decorating styles. You simply can't go wrong by choosing this window treatment for any room in your home.

Round Up

Now, let's get started and gather the following:
– Home dec sewing kit
– Decorator fabric*
– Lining fabric*
– Thread to match decorator fabric
– Shade cord
– Roman shade rings
– Cord drop (one)
– Screw eyes (four for a window up to 54 inches wide)
– Awning cleat (one)
– For slats: $1/4$-inch by $3/4$-inch screen molding (cut one inch shorter than the finished width of the shade)*
– 1-inch by 2-inch inch mounting board (cut the width measurement of the window)
– 2-inch screws (one for each end of the board and one for every 36 inches of board length)
– White fabric glue
*Calculated to fit your window.

Fabric Swap

Select a light- to medium-weight fabric and lining for this treatment. Do not use a heavy fabric. Choose quilt-weight cottons and light- to medium-

weight drapery cottons, silk, or damask. For the shade to hang nicely, it is very important that the fabric be tightly woven and that any design be printed on grain.

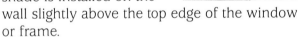

Before You Begin

You have two choices when making a Roman shade. An inside-mounted shade is installed within the frame of the window. An outside-mounted shade is installed on the wall slightly above the top edge of the window or frame.

Consider making an inside mount if you have handsome trim around the window or if you want your window to appear narrower. Consider an outside mount if you have nonexistent or unattractive window trim, if the window frame is not deep enough to contain a 1-inch by 2-inch mounting board (flat side up against the top inside edge of the window), or if you need to make a window appear wider.

Whatever decision you make, the construction method is exactly the same.

HOME DEC BECK SAYS:

"Select a fabric that you really want to show off. When the shade is lowered (even partially), the fabric becomes the star attraction."

PART 3
MAKE IT!

HOME DEC BECK SAYS:

"Wrap the mounting board with fabric just like you are wrapping a gift. Staple the fabric to the board as you wrap. Keep the fabric as smooth as possible, and trim away any excess fabric to eliminate bulk."

Go Figure

Need help measuring? Here's where to find it. How to Measure a Window, page 50

Refer to fig. 1 as you follow these easy calculations for the decorator and lining fabrics to make your shade. When planning an outside mount, allow enough room between the top edge of the window frame and the lower edge of the screw eyes (about 2 inches). The wide, flat side of the board is placed against the wall. For an inside mount, the flat side of the board is placed against the upper inside opening of the window (like a shelf) with the narrow edge facing front.

Note: The folds in this style of shade are formed by inserting slats of wood into evenly spaced

Fig. 1

horizontal channels that are stitched on the wrong side of the shade. Extra fabric is needed to accommodate these channels. The number of channels is based on your window size

1. Determine the placement of the mounting board. Measure from the top edge of the board to the top of the windowsill: ___. That's measurement A.

2. To determine the number of channels for your shade, draw a rectangle to represent your measurement (A) (fig. 2). Divide the length into sections as follows: mark the first line 6 inches up from the bottom edge; then mark parallel lines that are spaced 12 inches above the previous line. Mark as many 12-inch sections as possible. How many horizontal lines did you draw? ___

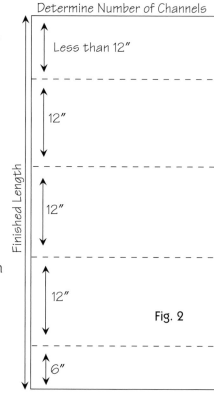

Determine Number of Channels

Finished Length

Less than 12"

12"

12"

12"

6"

Fig. 2

3. Multiply the above answer by $2\frac{1}{2}$ inches, that's measurement B: ___.

4. Add (A) and (B) together and add 5 inches. That's measurement C: ___. This is your cut-length measurement.

5. Now measure the distance across the board from end to end. To this number add $2\frac{1}{2}$ inches, that's measurement D: ___ . This is the cut-width measurement.

6. The width of your fabric is measurement E: ___.

7. Divide (D) by (E). Round up to the nearest whole number, that's measurement F: ___. This is the number of fabric widths to cut.

8. If (F) is greater than 1, continue with steps 9 through 12.

If (F) is not greater than 1, divide the cut length measurement (C) by 36 inches for the total yardage you need for both the decorator and lining fabrics. You're all done!

9. The fabric's repeat distance (if applicable) is measurement G: ___.

10. Divide the cut length (C) by the repeat distance (G) and round up to the nearest whole number. That's measurement H: ___.

11. Multiply the repeat distance (G) by (H) for measurement I: ___. This is the extra amount of fabric needed (in inches) to match the repeat. Add this number to your cut length measurement (C) for measurement J: ___.

12. Multiply the number of fabric widths you need to cut (F) by (J) and divide by 36 inches for the total yardage you need for both the decorator and lining fabrics: ___.

On the Cutting Edge

Before cutting into your beautiful fabric, review these cutting tips.
– Let's Get This Straight, page 53
– Fussy Cutting, page 55
– Repeat after Me, page 54
– Cut It Out, page 49

Straighten one end of the fabric. Cut one fabric width to the cut length measurement (C). Using this width as a guide, cut additional fabric widths (F). Don't forget to match the design repeats as you cut the additional fabric widths. Cut the same number of widths from the lining fabric.

Gearing Up

If you need help setting up your sewing machine, refer to page 42.

It's Sew Time!

Need to brush up on your sewing skills? Here's where to find help.
– Seam Team, page 42
– Pressing Matters, page 45
– Split Personality, page 56
– Matchmaking, page 57
– Cutting It Down to Size, page 57
– Go to the Corner, page 43

1. Stitch the decorator fabric widths right sides together, match repeats as necessary. Press the seams open. Repeat for the lining.

2. Trim equal amounts from both side edges of the decorator fabric to the cut width measurement (D) (fig. 3). Cut the lining fabric 2 inches narrower than the decorator fabric.

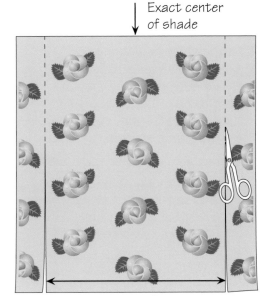

Fig. 3

Exact center of shade

Trim equal amounts from each side to cut width measurement

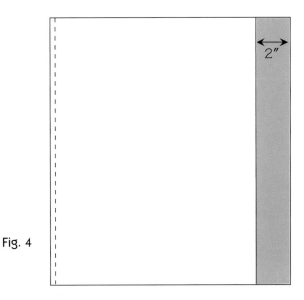

Fig. 4

2"

3. Place the fabric and lining right sides together; align the top, bottom, and one side edge. Stitch along this side edge (fig. 4).

4. Gently pull the lining to meet the opposite side of the decorator fabric and then stitch

(fig. 5), resulting in one large tube. Press both seams toward the decorator fabric.

5. On a large, flat surface, arrange the shade so the lining is centered and the decorator fabric is even on each side and the shade is straight and square. Stitch along the bottom edge (fig. 6).

6. Trim the corners diagonally and turn the shade right side out. The decorator fabric will wrap around to the back $^1/_2$ inch on each side (fig. 7). Press the shade smooth.

7. Along the bottom edge, turn up $1^1/_2$ inches toward the lining and press. Stitch along the top edge of the fold (fig. 8). This creates the bottom hem pocket where the screen molding is inserted, but do not insert it yet.

8. With the lining side up, measure up from the bottom hemmed edge of the shade $7^1/_4$ inches. Mark each side with a pin. With a fabric marker, draw a line across the width of the shade from pin to pin. Make sure this line is perpendicular to the side edges and parallel to the bottom edge (fig. 9).

9. From this drawn line, measure up $14^1/_2$ inches and draw another parallel line across the shade. Continue drawing parallel lines across the shade every $14^1/_2$ inches to equal the number of channels for your shade (fig. 10).

10. Working from the bottom to the top, fold the shade right sides together at the first line and press. With a fabric

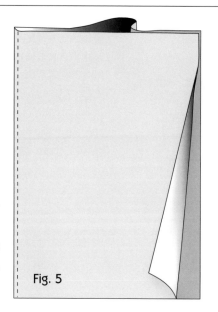
Fig. 5

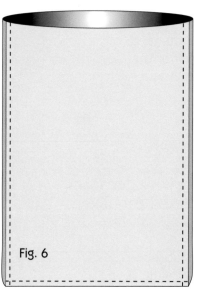
Fig. 6

Fig. 7

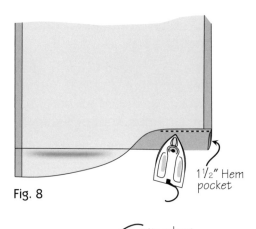
Fig. 8
1½" Hem pocket

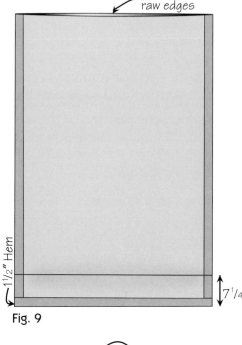
raw edges
1½" Hem
7¼"
Fig. 9

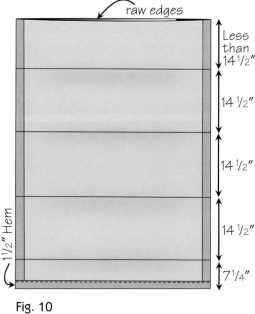
raw edges
Less than 14½"
14½"
14½"
14½"
1½" Hem
7¼"
Fig. 10

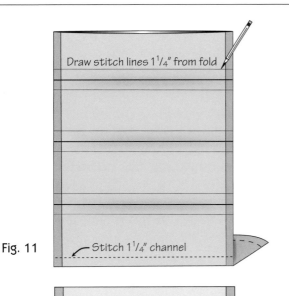

Fig. 11

Draw stitch lines 1¹/₄" from fold

Stitch 1¹/₄" channel

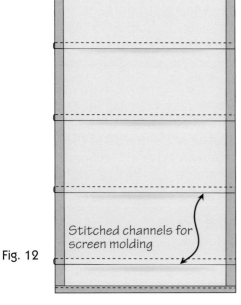

Fig. 12

Stitched channels for screen molding

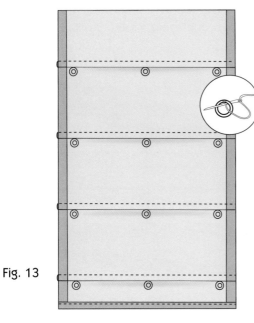

Fig. 13

marker, draw a line 1 $\frac{1}{4}$ inches from the fold. Machine stitch directly on top of this line (fig. 11). Repeat for the other channels (fig. 12). These channels are for the screen molding.

The Finish Line

Note: You can raise the shade from either the left or the right. The illustrations show a shade being rigged to raise from the left side. Reverse the instructions to raise shade from the right.

1. Handstitch one shade ring to the folded edge of each stitched channel 3 inches in from both sides and one directly in the center (fig. 13).

2. Cut the screen molding 1 inch shorter than the finished width of the shade. Cut a length of molding for each stitched channel plus one for the hem pocket.

3. Insert the screen molding into these channels and also the bottom hem pocket.

4. For an outside mount, attach two screw eyes, spaced 1 inch apart, to the narrow edge of the mounting board 2 and 3 inches in from one side (where you plan to raise the shade). Also attach one screw eye 3 inches in from the opposite side and one screw eye directly in the center of the board (fig 14).

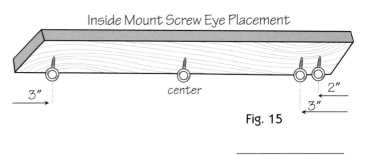

Outside Mount Screw Eye Placement

3"   center   2"   Fig. 14   3"

5. For an inside mount, attach the screw eyes, spaced 1 inch apart, to the wide, flat edge of the mounting board 2 and 3 inches in from the side. Also attach one screw eye 3 inches in from the opposite side (where you plan to raise the shade), and one screw eye directly in the center of the board (fig. 15).

Inside Mount Screw Eye Placement

3"   center   2"   3"   Fig. 15

PART 3 MAKE IT!

6. Staple the shade to the mounting board. For an inside mount, the shade is stapled to the wide, flat side that does not have the screw eyes inserted (fig. 16). For an outside mount, the shade covers the front of the board and is stapled to the flat side of the board that will be against the wall (fig. 17).

7. With a square knot, tie one end of shade cord to the bottom ring on one side of the shade. Thread the cord up through all the rings in the vertical row and across the board through all screw eyes (fig. 18). Repeat in the middle and on the other side. Dab some white fabric glue on the tied knot at each bottom ring to prevent it from coming undone. The ends of each cord should hang down one side about half the length of the shade.

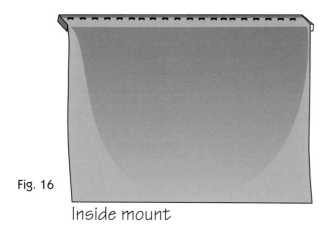

Fig. 16

Inside mount

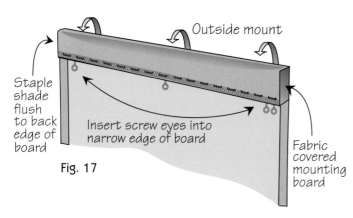

Outside mount

Staple shade flush to back edge of board

Insert screw eyes into narrow edge of board

Fabric covered mounting board

Fig. 17

Mounting the Shade

For an outside mount, install the mounting board above the window frame so the wide, flat side of the board with the staples is flush against the wall. Use a level when positioning the board. Screw the screws through the mounting board and into the wall.

For an inside mount, install the board against the inside of the window so the wide, flat side of the board is against the inside of the top of the frame and the narrow edge of the board faces out. Screw the screws vertically through the mounting board and directly into the window frame.

Tie Off the Cords

1. After the shade is installed, unfurl it completely.

2. Adjust the cords so that when they are pulled, the shade will draw up evenly (fig. 19).

3. While the shade is lowered, knot all the cords together just below the last screw eye.

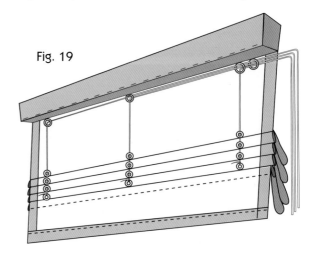

Fig. 19

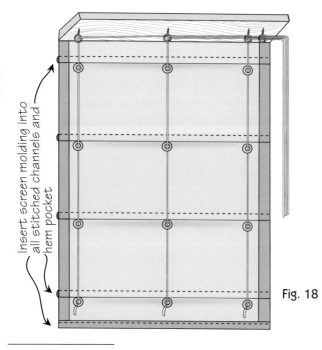

Insert screen molding into all stitched channels and hem pocket

Fig. 18

PART 3 MAKE IT!

4. Braid the cords together tightly. Insert the cord ends into a cord drop. This is a very important step for safety reasons. Dangling cords are a choking hazard for children and pets.

5. Attach a cord cleat to an inconspicuous place beside the window. Wrap the cords around the cleat to hold shade in place when the shade is lifted (fig. 20).

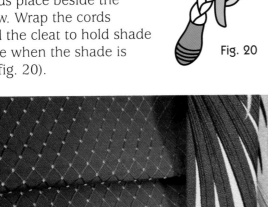

Fig. 20

▶ u dzine it

Since decorating is all about your individual style, here are some ideas for making a one-of-a kind Roman shade:

- Before the shade is lined, decorate the front of the shade with satin or grosgrain ribbon.

- Piece several different fabrics together to create a unique shade front.

- Use two fabrics in the same color family to create the shade front. Put one fabric in the center, the second at each side.

- Consider the shade front to be an artist's canvas and paint your own fabric design directly onto the fabric. Use specially designed fabric paints for this.

- Utilize those beautiful decorative stitches available on some sewing machines to create unique designs for your shade.

More Splash Than Cash®
Decorating Tips

Roman shades provide a clean, uncluttered look for any window in your home. The shade hangs perfectly flat when lowered (an opportunity to show off beautiful fabric) and folds up neatly at the top of the window when fully raised.

- A Roman shade is attractive enough to be a solo window treatment, yet it partners perfectly with sleek panel curtains. Instructions for making easy panel curtains are on pages 78 and 100.

An inside mounted Roman shade gives the window a sleek, neat look.

- Add a shelf above the window and display items that incorporate similar colors or textures that are in the shade fabric.

- Instead of using a structured valance to top the shade, add a decorative rod above the window and wrap and loop sheer fabric around the rod. Intertwine silk flowers and tiny white Christmas lights for a soft, romantic look.

PART 3
MAKE IT!

Glossary

What the #@&% Does This Mean?

Don't let an unfamiliar word or phrase cause you any frustration. I've compiled this quick mini-reference guide to help you

A

Apron – The bottom portion of a window frame that is flush against the wall.

Awl – A woodworking tool with a sharp point that creates holes in wood when tapped with a hammer.

B

Backstitch – A stitch used to secure the beginning and end of a row of machine stitching.

Ball fringe – A decorative trim constructed of fluffy dangling balls.

Baste – To sew a row of temporary stitches; can be done by machine or hand.

Batting – A fluffy substance used for padding; available in different thicknesses by the yard and prepackaged.

Bias – The 45-degree diagonal direction between the lengthwise and crosswise grains of fabric.

Blind stitch – A stitch used for hemming window treatments. It consists of several straight stitches, then a zigzag stitch that moves to the side and "bites" the fabric to hold the hem in place.

Bobbin – A spool-like thread holder that supplies the bottom thread for a machine stitch. It is placed in a compartment directly below the needle.

Bolt – Thick cardboard on which fabric is rolled to be displayed in a fabric store.

Broadcloth – A cotton fabric with a very fine crosswise thread. Similar to muslin in a solid color.

C

Café curtain – A half curtain that is hung from a rod that is mounted in the middle of a window.

Carpenter's square – An L-shaped measuring device that enables one to measure length and width simultaneously or to mark a 90-degree angle.

Carpet thread – Coarse, strong thread.

Clip – To make small scissor cuts into a seam allowance to allow movement of fabric—around a curve, for example.

Cord pull – A plastic cover used to hold multiple shade cords together.

Cover button – A form to be covered with fabric; it has a special backing that, once snapped in place, will form a button.

Crosswise grain – The threads that run perpendicular to the lengthwise grain and the selvage edge.

Cut length – This is how long you cut the fabric. This distance equals the vertical length measurement of the project plus any allowances for construction details such as seams or hems.

Cut width – This is the fabric measurement from side edge to side edge after the widths of fabric are stitched together but before any construction begins.

D

Damask – A firm jacquard-style fabric. Similar to brocade but reversible.

Decorator needle – An extra-long needle useful for attaching buttons through thick surfaces.

Decorator rod – Decorative hardware from which valances or curtains hang. These rods are meant to be visible.

Desired finished length – This is where you want the bottom edge of a valance or curtain to hang on the window.

Dupioni – An unevenly woven silk fabric.

Drapery rings – Wooden or metal rings that slide onto rods; they're secured to a window treatment with either stitches or an attached clip.

Dress goods – A term that refers to 45-inch-wide fabrics that are usually used for garments but can also be used in home decorating projects.

Dressing – The styling and positioning of the fabric in a window treatment.

Drill bit – A device inserted into a drill to make a hole in a wall or wooden surface.

Duck – A very durable, closely woven fabric of varying weights. Printed or solid.

Dye lot – A color run of fabric that may vary slightly in color from one batch to the next.

E

Ease – The extra amount of fabric or trim included in a measurement to ensure that it will not bind or be too small.

Edge stitch – To sew an even row of stitching along a pressed or seamed edge of fabric.

F

Fabric finishes – Processes that a fabric goes through to make it more durable, decorative, or serviceable. Finishes are usually applied with chemicals or mechanical pressure.

Fabric marker – A special temporary marker for fabrics that is removable by brushing off or applying water, or that is air soluble.

Face – The front or decorative side of fabric used for home furnishings.

Facing – A piece of fabric that is attached to an edge to conceal the raw edges and the wrong side of the fabric.

Feed dog – A toothed mechanism in a sewing machine that is under the needle and presser foot and moves the fabric when sewing.

Finger press – A technique of pressing a small section of fabric without an iron; fabrics are flattened and creased pressure between the thumb and forefinger.

Finial – An ornamental accent used at the end of a curtain rod.

Finished length – The measurement equal to the vertical length of an item (such as a curtain or duvet cover) after the top and bottom edges are finished.

Finished width – The horizontal measurement of an item after all seams and side edges are sewn.

Flat fold – The end pieces of fabric for sale that are not rolled onto a bolt but are stacked in piles. Usually sold at a discount price.

Flat trim – A simple flat trim. Often used as a topical decoration because it is stitched to the surface of an item. Also known as gimp or braid.

Focal point – The first item you want to see when entering a room (usually the largest architectural feature in the room).

Fray – The process where threads in a woven fabric come loose or unravel from the body of the fabric.

French seam – An enclosed seam finish used when both sides of the fabric will be seen or no lining will cover the wrong side.

Full width – The entire width of fabric measured from selvage edge to selvage edge.

Fullness – The amount of fabric that is arranged onto a rod to create curves or gathers in a window treatment. Fullness is calculated by multiplying the length of the rod by a number — usually $1\frac{1}{2}$, 2, $2\frac{1}{2}$, or 3 — but sometimes more. The number depends on the style of the window treatment.

Fuse baste – To temporarily hold two fabrics together with a temporary bonding agent and heat.

Fuse – To adhere two layers together with a bonding agent and heat (usually from an iron).

Fusible interfacing – A product ironed to the wrong side of fabric to add strength and body.

Fusible tape – See paper-backed fusible tape.

Fussy cutting – Cutting out a project by focusing on a selected design on a fabric instead of cutting randomly into the fabric.

G

Grain line – Refers to thread direction — lengthwise or crosswise. Any diagonal thread that intersects these two grain lines is known as bias.

Grommets – Large eyelets or metal or plastic rings pressed through fabrics.

H

Half-Width – The width of fabric cut in half parallel to the selvage edge

Handwheel – The round mechanism on the right side of a sewing machine that can be turned manually to raise and lower the needle.

Hem – The side or bottom edge of a window treatment that is turned under twice and stitched.

I

Inside mount – A mounting board installed inside the window frame rather than on the wall surrounding the window.

Installation – The process of securing window hardware or mounting boards to the wall with nails and screws.

Interfacing – A nonwoven or woven fabric that adds body to soft fabrics.

Iron – (verb) A sweeping motion with a hot iron over fabric to remove wrinkles from fabric. (noun) A piece of equipment that generates heat to smooth fabric.

J

Jacquard – The name of a loom that produces an intricately woven fabric with a raised design. Fabric produced from this kind of loom is also referred to by this name.

K

Kraft paper – Specialty paper available in craft stores that is brown in color and available on a roll.

L

Leading edge – The inside vertical edge of a curtain, the edge that leads or moves forward when the curtain is pulled closed.

Lengthwise grain – The fabric threads that are parallel to the selvage edge.

Level – A carpenter's tool used to determine if something is evenly positioned on a horizontal or vertical plane.

Lining – A solid (usually white or off-white) fabric sewn onto the back of a window treatment.

Liquid seam sealant – A liquid that, when applied to a cut edge of fabric, will eliminate fraying.

Loose fiberfill – A fluffy substance used as stuffing or filling in pillows.

M

Miter – The junction formed by joining or folding fabric to make an angle.

Motif – A single design or decorative pattern within a larger, overall design.

Mounting board – A 1-by-2-inch piece of wood to which a Roman shade is attached.

Muslin – An inexpensive plain-weave cotton fabric.

N

Nap – The directional raised fibers on a fabric surface.

O

On grain – Threads of fabric are woven at 90 degree angles and the fabric is printed straight on the crosswise threads.

Outside mount – A mounting board installed on the wall outside the window frame.

Overcast – A machine stitch that encases the raw edges of fabric to prevent the fabric from raveling. This can be accomplished with a zigzag stitch.

P

Paper-backed fusible tape – A tape available in various widths that has a coating of glue or adhesive on one side that is activated when heated with an iron. Used to hold two pieces of fabric together.

Pillow form – Premade shapes to insert into pillows to give pillows their characteristic dimension.

Pilot hole – A tiny hole that is drilled into a wall or wood prior to inserting a screw.

Plumb – Not crooked.

Point turner – A flat, pointed tool used to push out a point from the wrong side to the right side without damaging the fabric.

Preshrink – The process of removing any potential shrinkage in fabric before any construction process begins.

Press cloth – Fabric that is placed between an iron and decorator fabric for protection against scorching and iron shine.

Press – An up-and-down motion when the iron is applied to a surface and then lifted and moved to another location.

Presser foot – A sewing machine attachment that mounts behind the needle and is raised or lowered to hold fabric in place while sewing. Sewing machines often come with specialty feet, including piping or cording foot, a blind hem foot, and a buttonhole foot.

Projection – The distance a bracket and rod extends from the wall.

R

Raw edge – The cut edge of the fabric.

Repeat – The distance from an element on one motif to the same element on the next motif; usually measured along the selvage edge. The repeat is usually indicated with a "plus" sign on the selvage.

Return – The length of the end projection of a mounting board or the distance a rod bracket extends from the wall.

Right side – The pretty side of the fabric or the side of the fabric you want to see.

Rod – What a window treatment is placed on. Rods are placed in brackets that are installed above the window.

S

Sateen – A fabric with a smooth, lustrous, satiny finish constructed when long, smooth crosswise (weft) yarns float over four or eight lengthwise (warp) yarns.

Seam allowance – The area of fabric that extends from the stitching line to the cut outer edge of a sewn seam.

Seam gauge – A tool with a movable dial or slide to assist in measuring accurately.

Seam ripper – A small tool with a pointed hook at one end. The point is used to pick (or rip out) stitches from fabric. The inside curve of the hook is designed for cutting seams.

Selvage – The finished lengthwise edges of fabric that run down each side. Includes colored circles, and the name of the designer and the manufacturer. This is where you will also find markings to indicate a fabric repeat.

Shade cord – A firm, smooth nylon cord primarily used to rig Roman shades.

Shade rings – Individual plastic rings used to guide shade cord on the back of a Roman shade.

Shank – The small protruding loop on the underside of a button, used to attach the button to the project.

Sill length – The finished length of a window treatment where the bottom edge just touches the sill of a window.

Slip stitch – A hidden handstitch that connects two layers of fabric. Used mainly as a finishing stitch to close items such as pillows.

Straightedge – The edge of a ruler or measuring device that can easily be traced.

Stud – The wooden supports behind walls; the "bones" of a house.

T

Tabs – Extensions of fabric formed into loops or ties to hang a curtain from a curtain rod.

Template – A manufactured pattern used as a guide for drawing or tracing a predetermined shape.

Tension – The tightness of the top and bottom threads in a machine stitched seam. Controlled by a dial on the sewing machine that increases or decreases the pressure on the threads as they are fed through the machine. Machines have separate tension controls for the top thread and for the bottom (bobbin) thread.

Thread – String-like fiber used to hold fabric together. Many types are available for different fabrics and projects. All-purpose thread is recommended for the projects in this book.

Topstitch – Machine stitching on the right (top) side of an item for decorative or functional purposes, often along the edge.

V

Valance – A fabric top treatment for windows.

Velvet – A soft, pile fabric.

W

Wall anchor – Used to strengthen hollow walls. Weight-support devices that insert into a wall to form a brace where wood-framing studs are absent.

Waxed button thread – A thread that has had beeswax applied to the surface to strengthen it for handsewing. The addition of beeswax reduces the tendency for the thread to tangle and knot during the sewing process.

Wrong side – The side of fabric that will not be seen in a finished project.

Y

Yardage – The term used to describe the total amount of fabric needed for a project in one-yard (36 inch) increments.

Yardstick – A measuring device that is usually made from wood and is exactly one yard (36 inches) in length.

Z

Zigzag – A type of stitch where the needle swings left to right as it stitches, creating an evenly notched stitch. Particularly helpful to prevent fabric from fraying when stitched along the cut edge of the fabric.

Index